Personal Data

Name:

Address:

Phone Number:

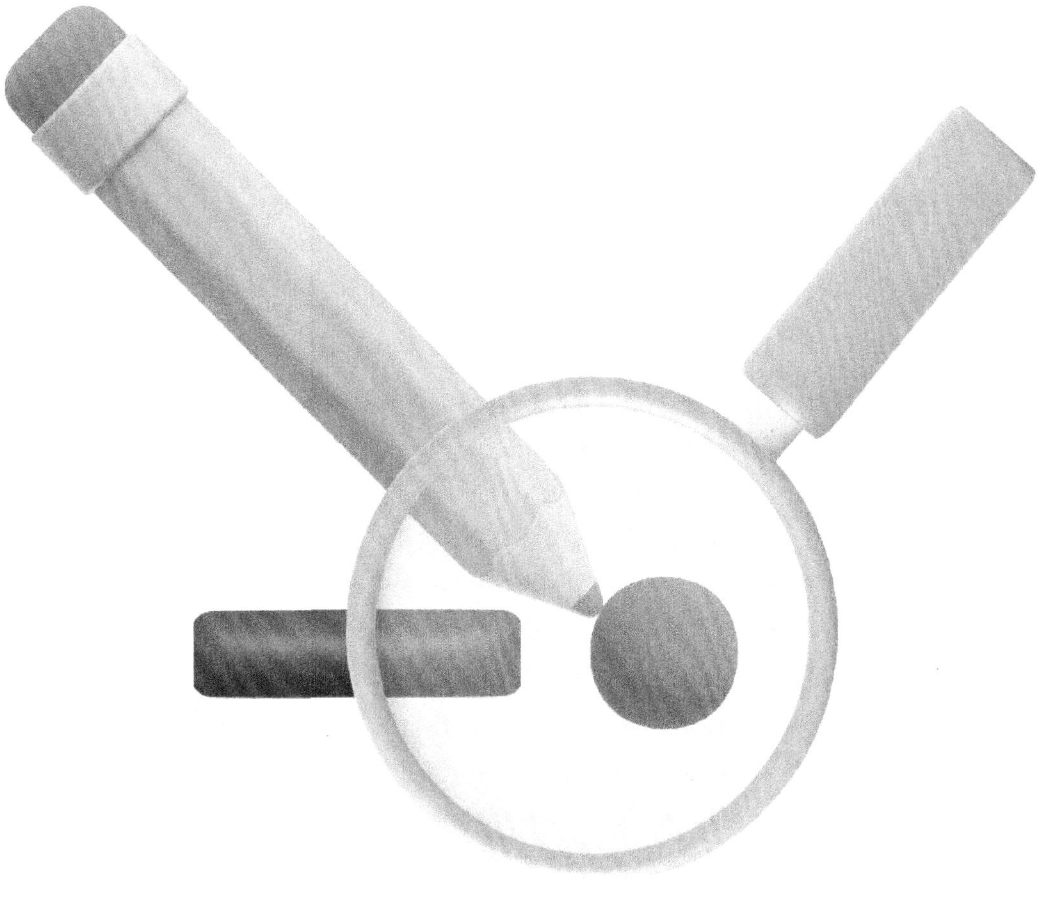

MORSE CODE

"In 1825 a painter named Samuel Morse. In Washington, D.C. Morse received a letter from his father -delivered via the standard, slow-moving horse messengers of the day- as his wife suddenly had suffered a heart attack while giving birth to their third child and she died, Morse immediately left the capital and hurried home in Connecticut. By the time he arrived, however, his wife wasn't only dead, she was already buried. He was so mad about the slow messages and distraught at the death of his wife, that he realized that we need a faster communication method and invented one. He called it Morse Code."

- Morse code is named for its inventor, Samuel Morse.
- The first official message to be sent in Morse code on a united states experimental telegraph line was relayed between Washington, D.C. and Baltimore, MD on May 24 ,1844.
- Morse code converts letters and numbers into a series of dots and dashes (sometimes called dits and dahs).
- In Morse code, each dash has a duration that is three times as long as each dot. Each dot or dash within a character is followed by a period of no signal, called a space, equal in duration to the dot.
- Morse code is well suited to be communicated through sound using audio tones. It can also be communicated visually using flashing lights or eye blinks.
- Although the code is not designed to be transmitted in written format, it can be written as well.

Morse Code rules

Morse code is a system of communication that used dots (.) and dashes and dashes (-).

A dot looks like a period (.) and a dash is a long horizontal line (-).

A dot is called a (dit or di), and a dash is called (dah).

The sound of a dit (.) is like (bep) and the sound of dah is like (beeep).

Morse Code rules:-

- The smallest unit in morse code is one unit.

- A dit is equal one unit.

- A dash is equal 3 units.

- The space between dits and dashes in the same letter is equal one unit (pause).

- The space between two letters in the same word is 3 units (pause).

- The space between two words is equal 7 units (pause) also a slash can be used instead of the 7 units of pause.

- There is no distinction between upper- and lower-case letters.

- For more understanding check the next message:

"I am Happy" in morse code is .. .- -- .... .- .--. .--. -.--

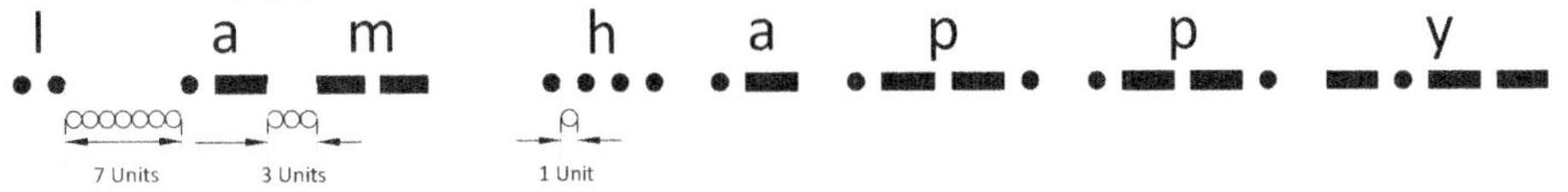

Also, the same sentence can be written with slashes between words as:

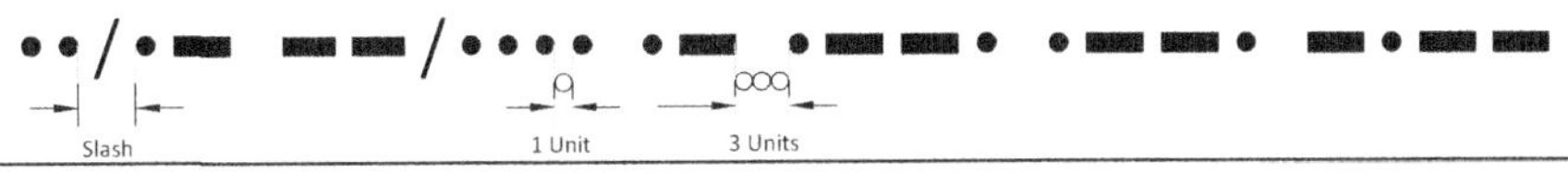

A	B	C	D	E	F	G	H	I
·−	−···	−·−·	−··	·	··−·	−−·	····	··
J	K	L	M	N	O	P	Q	R
·−−−	−·−	·−··	−−	−·	−−−	·−−·	−−·−	·−·
S	T	U	V	W	X	Y	Z	
···	−	··−	···−	·−−	−··−	−·−−	−−··	

1	2	3	4	5
·−−−−	··−−−	···−−	····−	·····
6	7	8	9	0
−····	−−···	−−−··	−−−−·	−−−−−
(		@		)
−·−−·		·−−·−·		−·−−·−
.	?	!	'	,
·−·−·−	··−−··	−·−·−−	·−−−−·	−−··−−
+	-	/	=	:
·−·−·	−····−	−··−·	−···−	−−−···

A .-

ALPHA

Phonetic

Match Letters to Morse Code

Some words are meaningless

[1] A	☐ .--
[2] AA	☐ .-
[3] A A	☐ .- .-
[4] W	☐ .- .-

Writing Practice

A .-	A .-
A .-	A .-

Read Aloud

A di dah
A di dah
A di dah
A di dah
A di dah
A di dah
A di dah
A di dah
A di dah
A di dah

Learned
A .- B C D E F G H I J K L M N O P Q R S T U V W X Y Z

T —

TANGO

Match Letters to Morse Code

1 T	☐ – –
2 M	☐ – –
3 TT	☐ ––
4 T T	☐ –

Writing Practice

T	AT ·– –
T –	AT ·– –

Read Aloud

T dah
T dah
T dah
T dah
T dah
AT di dah dah
AT di dah dah
AT di dah dah
AT di dah dah
AT di dah dah

Learned: A ·– B C D E F G H I J K L M N O P Q R S T – U V W X Y Z

E •

ECHO

Match Letters to Morse Code

1 E	☐ .-
2 EE	☐ . .
3 ET	☐ .
4 A	☐ . -

Writing Practice

E •

TEA ▬ • •▬

E •

TEA ▬ • •▬

Read Aloud

E dit

E dit

E dit

E dit

E dit

Tea dah di di dah

Tea dah di di dah

Tea dah di di dah

Tea dah di di dah

Tea dah di di dah

Learned A .- B C D E . F G H I J K L M N O P Q R S T - U V W X Y Z

M — — MIKE	**Match Letters to Morse Code** 1 M ☐ - - 2 TT ☐ --. 3 MM ☐ -- 4 G ☐ -- --

Writing Practice		Read Aloud	
M --	MEET -- . . -	M	dah dah
M --	MEET -- . . -	M	dah dah
		M	dah dah
		M	dah dah
		M	dah dah
		Me	dah dah dit
		Me	dah dah dit
		Me	dah dah dit
		Me	dah dah dit
		Me	dah dah dit

Learned

A .- B C D E . F G H I J K L M -- N O P Q R S T - U V W X Y Z

O ▬ ▬ ▬

OSCAR

Match Letters to Morse Code

1 O	☐ ---
2 MT	☐ --- ---
3 TM	☐ -- -
4 OO	☐ - --

Writing Practice

O ▬ ▬ ▬	TO - ---
O ▬ ▬ ▬	TO - ---

Read Aloud

O dah dah dah

O dah dah dah

O dah dah dah

O dah dah dah

O dah dah dah

To dah dah dah dah

To dah dah dah dah

To dah dah dah dah

To dah dah dah dah

To dah dah dah dah

Learned

A •▬ | B | C | D | E • | F | G | H | I | J | K | L | M ▬▬ | N | O ▬▬▬ | P | Q | R | S | T ▬ | U | V | W | X | Y | Z

The Learned Letters

A T E M O

Match Morse words with the correct Word

Mat		- . .- --
At		- ---
To		- . .-
Meat		.- -
Team		-- . .- -
Tea		-- .- -
Eat		. .- -

Match Morse words with the correct picture

- . .- --		
-- .- -		
- . .-		
. .- -		
-- . .- -		

Puzzle: Decode the learned letters and extract 5 words 🔍

-..-	-.-	.--	-.	.---	--..	-	---	--	--..	.-	-
...	.--	--	...-	.	.--.	.-	-.--	---	--.-	..	.--.
.---	.--	.	.--.	.-	.	.- A	-.	.	--.	-.-.	---
.---	...	.-	.--	-	-...	- T	-.-	.-.	-..-	-..	-.-.
.-	.--	-	.--	---	-.	-.-	--	.	--	.	..-.
-	-	.	.-	--	-..-	-.	.-	--..	-	---	.-..
.	--..	-.-	--	.-	--.-	-.-	-	-.-	.---	.---	.-
-.-.	....	-	-	--	-...	--..	- T	. E	.- A	.-.	-.-.

Translate text to Morse code

To	
At	
Team	
Me	
Tea	
Atom	

N -•

NOVEMBER

Match Letters to Morse Code

1 N	☐ .-
2 A	☐ .- .-
3 AA	☐ -.
4 NN	☐ -. -.

Writing Practice

N -•   NO -. ---

N -•   NO -. ---

Read Aloud

N dah dit

N dah dit

N dah dit

N dah dit

N dah dit

Extract the letter "N" and circle it:-(4)

.- .-. . / -.-- --- ..- /

..-. .-. . . / --- -. /

... ..- -. -.. .- -.-- /

.- ..-. - . .-. -. --- --- -.

Learned: A .- E . M -- N -. O --- T -

A B C D E F G H I J K L M N O P Q R S T U V W X Y Z

S •••

SIERRA

Match Letters to Morse Code

1 S	☐ ••• •••
2 SS	☐ • • •
3 S S	☐ ••• •••
4 EEE	☐ •••

Writing Practice

S •••   SOS ••• --- •••

S •••   SOS ••• --- •••

Read Aloud

S di di dit

S di di dit

S di di dit

S di di dit

S di di dit

Extract the letter "S" and circle it:-(3)

•• / •- -- /

••• •-- - •• ••• ••-• •• • -•• /

•-- •• - •••• / - •••• • /

••• • •-• •••- •• -•-• •

Learned: A E M N O S T

I ••

INDIA

Match Letters to Morse Code

1 I	☐ ••
2 IE	☐ •• •
3 S	☐ • ••
4 EI	☐ •••

Writing Practice

I •• | Tie - •• •

I •• | Tie - •• •

Read Aloud

i di dit

i di dit

i di dit

i di dit

i di dit

Extract the letter "I" and circle it:-(2)

•• / •- -- / --• --- •• -• --• /

- --- / - •••• • /

•-•• •• -••• •-• •- •-• -•--

Learned

A •- E • I •• M -- N -• O --- S ••• T -

R •▬•

ROMEO

Match Letters to Morse Code

1 R	☐ .-.
2 EN	☐ .- .
3 AE	☐ . -.
4 ETE	☐ . - .

Writing Practice

R •▬• RAT .-. .- -

R •▬• RAT .-. .- -

Read Aloud

R di dah dit

R di dah dit

R di dah dit

R di dah dit

R di dah dit

Extract the letter "R" and circle it:-(3)

.- .-. . / -.-- --- ..- /

..-. .-. . . / --- -. /

... ..- -. -.. .- -.-- /

.- ..-. - . .-. -. --- --- -.

Learned: A .- E . I .. M -- N -. O --- R .-. S ... T -

B C D F G H J K L P Q U V W X Y Z

H ....

HOTEL

Match Letters to Morse Code

1	H	☐	.. ...
2	IS	☐	.. ..
3	SI	☐	....
4	II	☐	... ..

Writing Practice

H ....

HAT .... .- -

H ....

HAT .... .- -

Read Aloud

H di di di dit

H di di di dit

H di di di dit

H di di di dit

H di di di dit

Extract the letter "H" and circle it:-(3)

.... --- .-- / -- .- -. -.-- /

-.-. ....-.. -.. .-. . -. /

-.. --- / -.-- --- ..- /

.... .- ...- .

Learned

A .- B C D E . F G H .... I .. J K L M -- N -. O --- P Q R .-. S ... T - U V W X Y Z

The Learned Letters

A E M O T N S I R H

Match Morse words with the correct Word

Ant		-- .- -.
Arm		.- -. -
Man		... -- .- .-. -
Smart		.- .-. --
Nine		- . -.
ten		.... . -.
Hen		-. .. -. .

Match Morse words with the correct picture

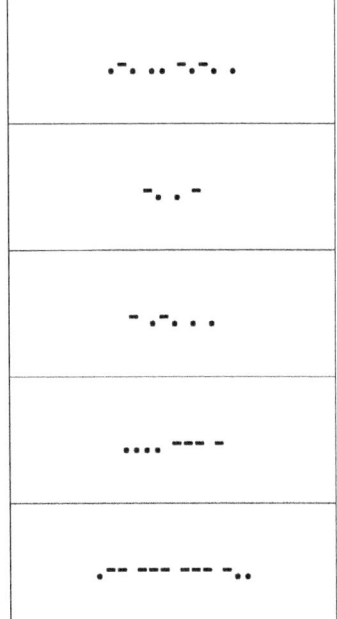

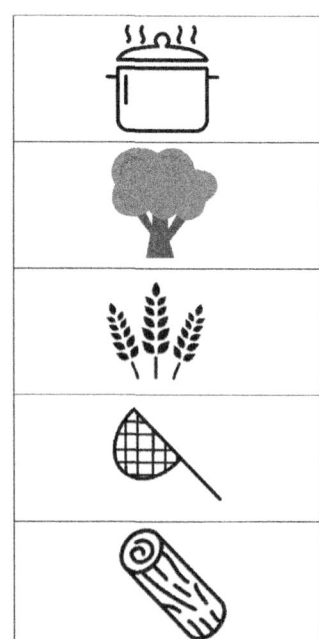

.-. .. -.-. .		
-. . -		
- .-. . .		
.... --- -		
.-- --- --- -..		

Puzzle: Decode the learned letters and extract 7 words 🔍

--	-	.--	.	.-	-	-..-	--.	-.	.-	.-.	.--.
-	.	-	-.-	-	.	-.	--.-	.	-	..-.	..-.
.--	.-	-. N	.. I	-. N	. E	...	--.-	-	-.--	.-	--.-
--..	.-.	-.-	-.	---	-...	...	.-	--.-	..-.	-..-	.--.
--	....	--	.-	....	...	--	.-	.-.	-	...	..-.
.-	---	...-	--	--.-	.-	-.	-	-	---	.-..	-.-
-	-	..	.	--.-	...	-.-.	--.	....	.-	-	--.
.--	....	.	-.	-.	-	.	.-	--	.-.	-...	--..

Translate text to Morse code

Wood	
Tree	
Car	
Rice	
Arm	
Man	

D -..

DELTA

Match Letters to Morse Code

1 D	☐ -. .
2 NE	☐ -..
3 TI	☐ - ..
4 TEE	☐ - . .

Writing Practice

D -.. DO -.. ---

D -.. DO -.. ---

Read Aloud

D dah di dit

D dah di dit

D dah di dit

D dah di dit

D dah di dit

Extract the letter "D" and circle it:-(4)

.-- .... . -. / -.. .. -.. /

-.-- --- ..- / --. . - /

-.. .. ...- --- .-. -.-. . -..

Learned

A .- B C D -.. E . F G H .... I .. J K L M -- N -. O --- P Q R .-. S ... T - U V W X Y Z

L •▬••

LIMA

Match Letters to Morse Code

1 L	☐ .-. .
2 RE	☐ . -. .
3 ENE	☐ . - ..
4 ETI	☐ .-..

Writing Practice

L .-.. LOT .-.. --- -

Read Aloud

L di dah di dit

L di dah di dit

L di dah di dit

L di dah di dit

L di dah di dit

Extract the letter "L" and circle it:-(3)

.... --- .-- / .-.. --- -. --. /

.. ... / - .... . /

. -. --. .-.. .. .. /

-.-. .-.. .- ... ...

Learned: A .- D -.. E . H .... I .. L .-.. M -- N -. O --- R .-. S ... T -

U •• ▬

UNIFORM

Match Letters to Morse Code

1 U	☐ ..-
2 EA	☐ . . -
3 IT	☐ . .-
4 EET	☐ .. -

Writing Practice

U •• ▬ Unit ..- -. .. -

U •• ▬ Unit ..- -. .. -

Read Aloud

U di di dah

U di di dah

U di di dah

U di di dah

U di di dah

Extract the letter "U" and circle it:-(3)

.-- --- ..- .-.. -.. / -.-- --- ..- /

.--. .-.. . .- ... . /

.-- .- -.- . / -- . /

..- .--. / .- - / --... .- --

⊘Learned A B C D E F G H I J K L M N O P Q R S T U V W X Y Z

C -.-.

CHARLIE

Match Letters to Morse Code

1 C	☐ -. -.
2 NN	☐ - . - .
3 TETE	☐ -.-.
4 TR	☐ - .-.

Writing Practice

C -.-.	Cat -.-. .- -
C -.-.	Cat -.-. .- -

Read Aloud

C dah di dah dit

C dah di dah dit

C dah di dah dit

C dah di dah dit

C dah di dah dit

Extract the letter "C" and circle it:-(3)

.. / .-.. .. -.- . /

-.-. .... --- -.-. --- .-.. .- - . /

-.-. .- -.- .

Learned: A .- C -.-. D -.. E . H .... I .. L .-.. M -- N -. O --- R .-. S ... T - U ..-

W •▬▬

WILLIAM

Match Letters to Morse Code

1 W	☐ . --
2 AT	☐ .- -
3 EM	☐ . - -
4 ETT	☐ .--

Writing Practice

W •▬▬ What .-- .... .- -

W •▬▬ What .-- .... .- -

Read Aloud

W dit dah dah

W dit dah dah

W dit dah dah

W dit dah dah

W dit dah dah

Extract the letter "W" and circle it:-(2)

.... --- .-- / -.. --- /

-.-- --- ..- / --. . - /

- --- / .-- --- .-. -.-

Learned

A .- B C -.-. D -.. E . F G H .... I .. J K L .-.. M -- N -. O --- P Q R .-. S ... T - U ..- V W .-- X Y Z

The Learned Letters

A E M O T N S I R H D L U C W

Match Morse words with the correct Word

AIR		.- .. .-.
LAW		.-.. .- .--
WIN		- .-. . .
TREE		.-- .. -.
DUCK		.-.. ..- -.-. -.-
LUCK		.-- --- .-. -..
WORD		-.. ..- -.-. -.-

Match Morse words with the correct picture

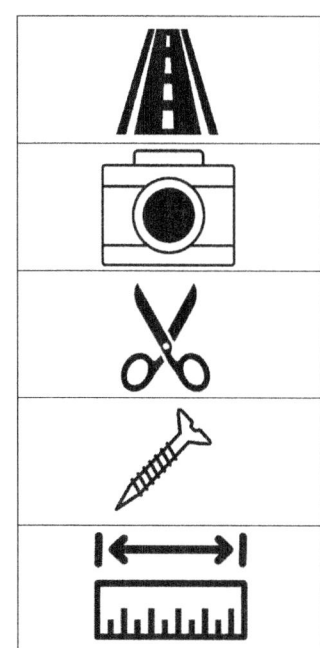

... -.-. .. .. --- .-. ...		
... -.-. .-. . .--		
.-. --- .- -..		
.-. ..- .-.. . .-.		
-.-. .- -- . .-. .-		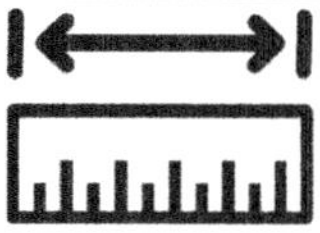

Puzzle: Decode the learned letters and extract 10 words🔍

.-	-.-	.-.	..-.	-.-.	.-	.--	.--.	...-	--.-	-	--
-.	.-..	.-..	.-.	..	-.-.	.	-	.-.	.	.	.-
..	-.-.	.-	-	---	.--.	.--	..	-.	.-..	--.-	-.
--	.--	.--	--	.	.-	-	.---	--.	.	.--	.-
.-	-.-.	.-.	.-	.-.	--	.-..	---	.--	-.	---	.-.
.-..	.-.	---	.-	-..	-...	..-	..-.	-.-.	...	.-.	-.-.
..-.	-.-.	.-	.-.	..	.--	---	---	-..	...-	-..	--..
-.	..	-.	.	.-	..	.-.	..	-.-.	.	.-.	-..-

Translate text to Morse code

AIR	
LENS	
WORD	
LAW	
ROAD	
CAW	

F ..-.

FOXTROT

Match Letters to Morse Code

1 F	☐ . .-.
2 ER	☐ ..-.
3 ITE	☐ .. -.
4 IN	☐ .. - .

Writing Practice

F ..-. Fat ..-. .- -

F ..-. Fat ..-. .- -

Read Aloud

F di di dah dit

F di di dah dit

F di di dah dit

F di di dah dit

F di di dah dit

Extract the letter "F" and circle it:-(2)

.-- .... .- - / -.-. .. -. -.. /

--- ..-. / ..-. --- --- -.. /

-.. --- / -.-- --- ..- /

.-.. .. -.- .

Learned

A .- | C -.-. | D -.. | E . | F ..-. | H .... | I .. | L .-.. | M -- | N -. | O --- | R .-. | S ... | T - | U ..- | W .--

Match Letters to Morse Code

1 Y	☐ -. --
2 TAT	☐ -.--
3 TETT	☐ - .- -
4 NM	☐ - . - -

Y -.--

YANKEE

Writing Practice

Y -.-- You -.-- --- ..-

Y -.-- You -.-- --- ..-

Read Aloud

Y dah di dah dah

Y dah di dah dah

Y dah di dah dah

Y dah di dah dah

Y dah di dah dah

Extract the letter "Y" and circle it:-(2)

-- -.-- / ..-. .-. .. . -. -.. /

.. ... / ..-. .-. --- -- /

. --. -.-- .--. -

Learned

A .- C -.-. D -.. E . F ..-. H .... I .. L .-.. M -- N -. O --- R .-. S ... T - U ..- W .-- Y -.--

P •▬▬•

PAPA

Match Letters to Morse Code

1 P	☐ .--.
2 R	☐ .-.
3 AN	☐ . -- .
4 EME	☐ .- -.

Writing Practice

P •▬▬• Pay .--. .- -.--

P •▬▬• Pay .--. .- -.--

Read Aloud

P dit dah dah dit

P dit dah dah dit

P dit dah dah dit

P dit dah dah dit

P dit dah dah dit

Extract the letter "P" and circle it:-(2)

.. / .-- --- .-. -.- /

.. -. / .- / .--. .- .--. . .-. /

..-. .- -.-. - --- .-. -.--

Learned

A	C	D	E	F	H	I	L	M	N	O	P	R	S	T	U	W	Y
.-	-.-.	-..	.	..-.	....	..	.-..	--	-.	---	.--.	.-.	...	-	..-	.--	-.--

G ▬ ▬ •

GOLF

Match Letters to Morse Code

1 G	☐ -- .
2 TTE	☐ - -.
3 ME	☐ --.
4 TN	☐ - - .

Writing Practice

G ▬▬•	Go --. ---
G ▬▬•	Go --. ---

Read Aloud

G dah dah dit

G dah dah dit

G dah dah dit

G dah dah dit

G dah dah dit

Extract the letter "G" and circle it:-(2)

--. --- --- -.. /

-- --- .-. -. .. -. --.

Learned: A •▬ C ▬•▬• D ▬•• E • F ••▬• G ▬▬• H •••• I •• L •▬•• M ▬▬ N ▬• O ▬▬▬ P •▬▬• R •▬• S ••• T ▬ U ••▬ W •▬▬ Y ▬•▬▬

B -...

BRAVO

Match Letters to Morse Code

1 B	☐ -...
2 NI	☐ -. ..
3 NEE	☐ -. . .
4 TIE	☐ - .. .

Writing Practice

B -... Bat -... .- -

B -... Bat -... .- -

Read Aloud

B dah di di dit

B dah di di dit

B dah di di dit

B dah di di dit

B dah di di dit

Extract the letter "F" and circle it:-(2)

.-- .... .- - / -.-. .. -. -.. /

--- ..-. / ..-. --- --- -.. /

-.. --- / -.-- --- ..- /

.-.. .. -.- .

Learned

A .- B -... C -.-. D -.. E . F ..-. G --. H .... I .. J K L .-.. M -- N -. O --- P .--. Q R .-. S ... T - U ..- V W .-- X Y -.-- Z

The Learned Letters

A	E	M	O	T	N	S	I	R	H	D	L	U	C	W	F	Y	P	G	B

Match Morse words with the correct Word

FAMILY	--. .- -- .
GYM	.- .--. .--. .-.. .
PEACE	.--. . .- -.-. .
SISTER	..-. .- -- .. .-.. -.--
APPLE	... . - . .-.
GAME	--. -.-- --
GIRL	--. .. .-. .-..

Match Morse words with the correct picture

-.-. ..- .--.	
.- .--. .--. .-.. .	
-- ..- --.	
-... ..- .-.. -...	
-... .- --.	

Puzzle: Decode the learned letters and extract 10 words 🔍

--.	..-.	.--.	.	.-	-.-.	.	..-	-..	-.-.	-..-	.-
.-	---	.-	.--.	.--.	.-..	.	...	..-.	..-	.---	..-.
--	---	--.	-.-.	.-..	..-	-...	..	.-	.--.	..-.	.-..
.	-..	..-	--.-	-..	---	--.	...	-	--.	.-..	.-
..-.	.-	--	..	.-..	-.--	-...	-	....	-.--	-.--	--
.--.	--	..-	--.	-...	---	-.--	.	.	--	.---	-...
--.	..	.-.	.-..	--	.-	.--.	.-.	.-.	--..	.-	....
..	.--.	-.-.	.-	-	...	--	.-	.-.	-	..-.	-...

Translate text to Morse code

MUG	
BAG	
CUP	
FLY	
Girl	
BROTHER	

V •••▬

VICTOR

Match Letters to Morse Code

1 V	☐ ...-
2 IA	☐ . ..-
3 EIT	☐ .. .-
4 EU	☐ . .. -

Writing Practice

V •••▬ Vat ...- .- -

V •••▬ Vat ...- .- -

Read Aloud

V di di di dah

V di di di dah

V di di di dah

V di di di dah

V di di di dah

Extract the letter "B" and circle it:-(1)

.. / .- -- /

.-. . .- -.. .. -. --. / .- /

-... --- --- -.-

Learned A B C D E F G H I J K L M N O P Q R S T U V W X Y Z

K -.-

KILO

Match Letters to Morse Code

1	K	☐	- .-
2	NT	☐	-. -
3	TET	☐	- . -
4	TA	☐	-.-

Writing Practice

K -.- Kit -.- .. -

K -.- Kit -.- .. -

Read Aloud

K dah di dah

K dah di dah

K dah di dah

K dah di dah

K dah di dah

Extract the letter "K" and circle it:-(2)

.. / .-. .. -.. . /

-- -.-- / -... .. -.- . /

- --- / .-- --- .-. -.-

Learned

A B C D E F G H I J K L M N O P Q R S T U V W X Y Z

J .---

JULIETT

Match Letters to Morse Code

1	J	☐	.- --
2	EMT	☐	.---
3	EO	☐	. -- -
4	AM	☐	. ---

Writing Practice

J .--- Jar .--- .- .-.

J .--- Jar .--- .- .-.

Read Aloud

J di dah dah dah

J di dah dah dah

J di dah dah dah

J di dah dah dah

J di dah dah dah

Extract the letter "J" and circle it:-(1)

.. / . -. .--- --- -.-- /

- .... / .--. . .- -.-. . /

.- -. -.. / --.- ..- .. . -

Learned

A B C D E F G H I J K L M N O P Q R S T U V W X Y Z

X -..-

X-RAY

Match Letters to Morse Code

1 X	☐ -. .-
2 NA	☐ -..-
3 TIT	☐ - .. -
4 DT	☐ -.. -

Writing Practice

X -..- Fox ..-. --- -..-

X -..- Fox ..-. --- -..-

Read Aloud

X dah di di dah

X dah di di dah

X dah di di dah

X dah di di dah

X dah di di dah

Extract the letter "X" and circle it:-(1)

.. / .-- .. .-.. .-.. / --. --- /

... . --- .--. .--. .. -. --. /

-. . -..- - / .-- . . -.-

Learned A B C D E F G H I J K L M N O P Q R S T U V W X Y Z

Q -- -- · --

QUEBEC

Match Letters to Morse Code

1 Q	☐ -- .-
2 MA	☐ --. -
3 GT	☐ - -.-
4 TK	☐ --.-

Writing Practice

Q --.- Queen --.- ..- . . -.

Q --.- Queen --.- ..- . . -.

Read Aloud

Q dah dah di dah

Q dah dah di dah

Q dah dah di dah

Q dah dah di dah

Q dah dah di dah

Extract the letter "Q" and circle it:-(1)

.. / . -. .--- --- -.-- /

- .... / .--. . .- -.-. . /

.- -. -.. / --.- ..- .. . -

Learned

A	B	C	D	E	F	G	H	I	J	K	L	M	N	O	P	Q	R	S	T	U	V	W	X	Y	Z
.-	-...	-.-.	-..	.	..-.	--.	....	..	.---	-.-	.-..	--	-.	---	.--.	--.-	.-.	...	-	..-	...-	.--	-..-	-.--	

Z ▬ ▬ • •

ZULU

Match Letters to Morse Code

1 Z	☐ - -. .
2 MI	☐ --. .
3 TNE	☐ --..
4 GE	☐ -- ..

Writing Practice

Z ▬▬•• Zebra --.. . -... .-. .-

Z ▬▬•• Zebra --.. . -... .-. .-

Read Aloud

Z dah dah di dit

Z dah dah di dit

Z dah dah di dit

Z dah dah di dit

Z dah dah di dit

Extract the letter "Z" and circle it:-(1)

.. - / .. ... /

..-. .-. . . --.. .. -. --. /

- --- -.. .- -.--

Learned

A	B	C	D	E	F	G	H	I	J	K	L	M	N	O	P	Q	R	S	T	U	V	W	X	Y	Z
.-	-...	-.-.	-..	.	..-.	--.	....	..	.---	-.-	.-..	--	-.	---	.--.	--.-	.-.	...	-	..-	...-	.--	-..-	-.--	--..

The Learned Letters

A	E	M	O	T	N	S	I	R	H	D	L	U	C	W	F	Y	P	G	B	V	K	J	X	Q	Z

Match Morse words with the correct Word

ANIMAL	.-.. .. --- -.
DUCK	.- -. .. -- .- .-..
LION	.--- ..- -. --. .-.. .
JUNGLE	-.. ..- -.-. -.-
JUMP	.--- ..- -- .--.
ZEBRA	--.- ..- .- .-.. .. - -.--
QUALITY	--.. . -... .-. .-

Match Morse words with the correct picture

-.- .. - .	
.--. ..- --.. --.. .-.. .	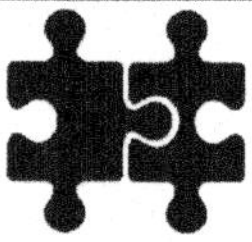
-... --- -..-	
--.- .-. --- .-- -.	
...- .-	

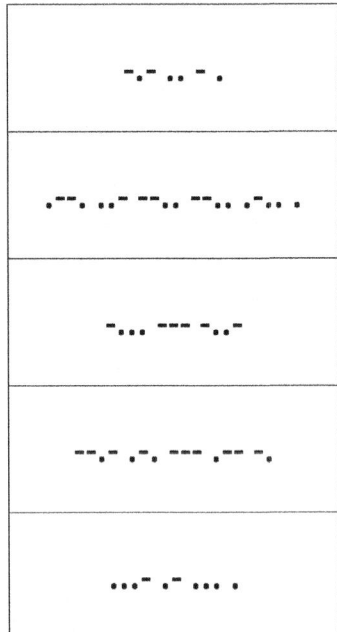

Puzzle: Decode the learned letters and extract 15 words

--..	...-	...-	-	.--	---	.-.	-..	--	..-	-.-	-...
---	.-	.-	--	---	.-.	...	.	.--.	-..	..	-...
---	...	-.	-..	-.--	.	.-..	.-..	---	.--	-	-.-
--..	.	-...	.-.	.-	..	-.-.	.	-...	-..-	.	..
...	--	.-	.-.	-	--.	.-	.--.	.--.	.-..	.	-.
-...	---	-..-	.-	-.	-	-	.---	.-	.-.	-..	--.
..-.	---	-..-	-	.--	.--	..	-.	-.	.	.-.	-..
--..	...-	--	---	.-.	...	.	-.-.	---	-..	.	...-

Translate text to Morse code

KING	
PUZZLE	
FOX	
JAR	
QUIZ	
VASE	

The Learned Letters

A B C D E F G H I J K L M N O P Q R S T U V W X Y Z

Match Morse words with the correct Word

Passenger	.--. --- .-- . .-.
Students	. -- . .-. --. . -. -.-. -.--
Power	..-. --- .-. --. . -
Emergency	.-- . .- - .... . .-.
Bee	.. -- .--. --- .-. - .- -. -
Forget	.-. --- -.-. -.- . -
Confidential	- --- --. . - .... . .-.
Weather	-. --- - . -... --- --- -.-
Together	.--. .- ... . -. --. . .-.
Spring	-... . .
Rocket	-.-. --- -. ..-. .. -.. . -. - .. .- .-..
Danger	... . -.-. .-. . -
Important	-.. .- -. --. . .-.
Secret	... - ..- -.. . -. - ...
Notebook	... .--. .-. .. -. --.

Puzzle: Decode the learned letters and extract 15 words 🔍

--	.	..-.	-.--	---	.--.	.	.-	-.-.	.	.---	-.-
.-	--.-	.-..	.	.-	-	....	.	-.	.-.	..-.	..
-	-	-.--	.-..	-.-.	..-	.--.	...	.-	-.-	--.-	-
-	.	.-	.-..	..	.-.	..	-.-.	.	..	....	.
....	-.	---	---	-.-.	.-..	.	-.	...	-.	.-	-.-.
--	..-	--.	.--	.	....	---	-	.--	--.	-	...
-.-.	.-	.--	--	.-	.--.	.--.	...-	.-	...	.	-.--
--..	---	---	--	.	.-	-	-..	--.	-.--	--	.--.

Date / /

A	B	C	D	E	F	G	H	I	J	K	L	M
·–	–···	–·–·	–··	·	··–·	––·	····	··	·–––	–·–	·–··	––

N	O	P	Q	R	S	T	U	V	W	X	Y	Z
–·	–––	·––·	––·–	·–·	···	–	··–	···–	·––	–··–	–·––	––··

ACTIVITY FOR KIDS

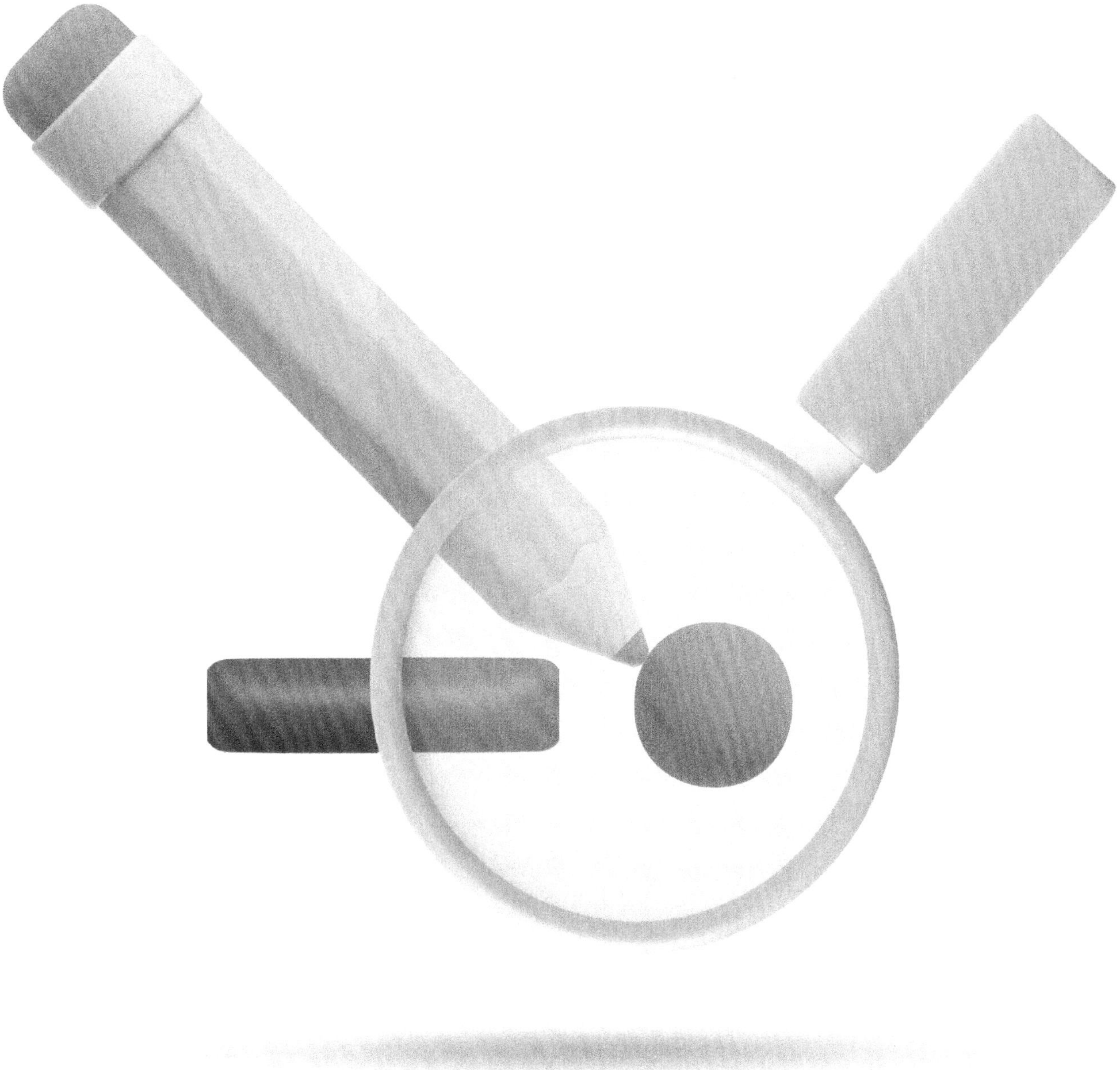

CIPHER WHEEL

Make a cipher wheel and use it to send secret messages to your friends and family.

The cipher is a code used to protect information that is being stored or communicated, so that only people who are allowed can access it those who have the code key.

This activity involves making a cipher wheel and using it to encrypt and decrypt messages with your friend or with your family, with a simple cipher made of paper.

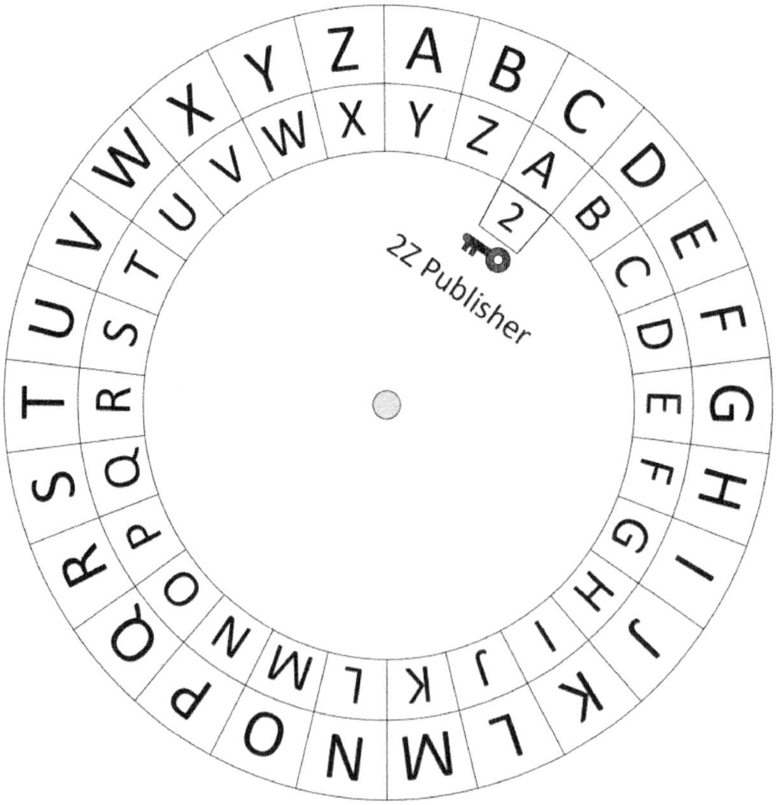

What this activity is?

Using the cipher wheel to encrypt a message -make it secret- involves transforming each letter of the message into another letter or a number by following a series of steps:

In this case, encrypting a message involves simply shifting each letter of the message by a certain number of places through the alphabet.

The message's receiver is aware of the encryption key– which, in the case of cryptography, is called a cipher – and can decrypt the messages by applying the process in reverse (decoding the secret message).

Needed Tools:

1. Pencil for making notes and writing messages.
2. Split Pin Paper Fasteners
   (Paper fasteners can be replaced by blue tack and wooden skewer).
3. Card Stock circles with the same size of templates
   (To make the cipher wheel rigid and last longer).
4. Glue (To stick the wheel to the Card stock).
5. Plastic Scissors.
6. Cipher Wheel templates (3 Copies are included for free in this book for our little heroes).

Follow these steps...

1. Cut the templates with the help of your parents.
2. Cut the card stock circles with the help of your parents.
3. Glue the Cipher wheel templates to the card stock circles.
4. Put the small circle on the large circle and secure it with a split pin in the center.
5. Choose a "key" or "shift", The number of letters the alphabet will be shifted by.
   E.g., with a shift of **2** A becomes C.
6. Rotate the front disc until the chosen shift is set. The shift number will appear in the "Key" window so that each letter on smaller Wheel lines up with a different letter on the larger wheel.
7. Now encrypt your message (make it secret).
   For each letter, write down the letter on the larger wheel that appears directly beneath it.
8. Don't forget to record your secret key.
   Either as the shift number as A=C for Key=**3** as you will need it to decode your secret message.
9. Encrypt messages to a friend in letters, and ask them to send you encrypted messages too, and their secret keys.
10. There are additional 2 copies of these templates in the last papers of this book so you can gift it to your loved friends or to family members to play together and enjoy this activity.

Scan QR Code for more understanding

(YouTube playlist that contains **2** Videos)

Try to encrypt next messages:

- I enjoy learning Morse code.
- Keep our secret.
- I love my family.
- Hello my friend.
- The enemy base is in the north.

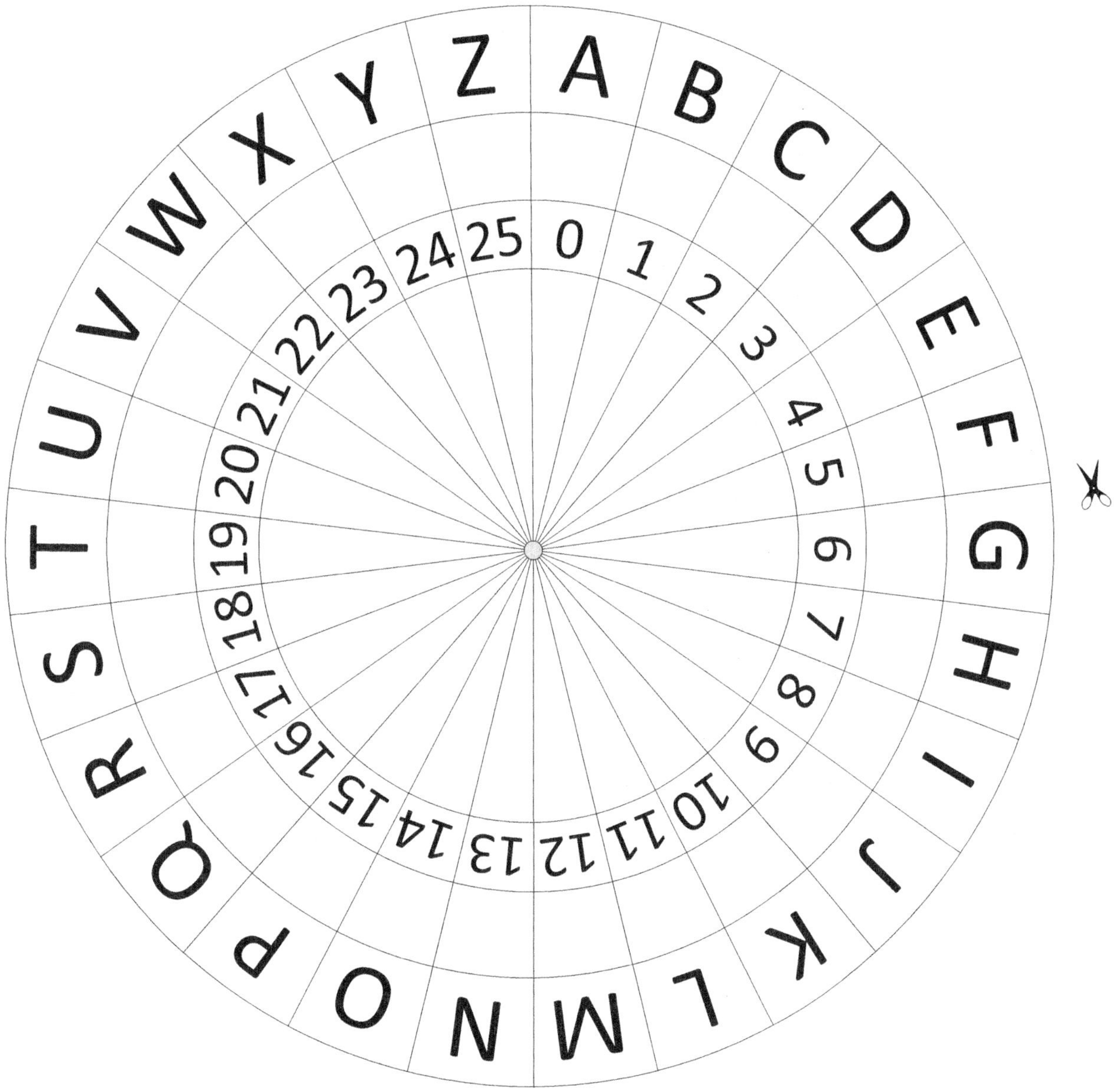

Template.1 (Large circle)

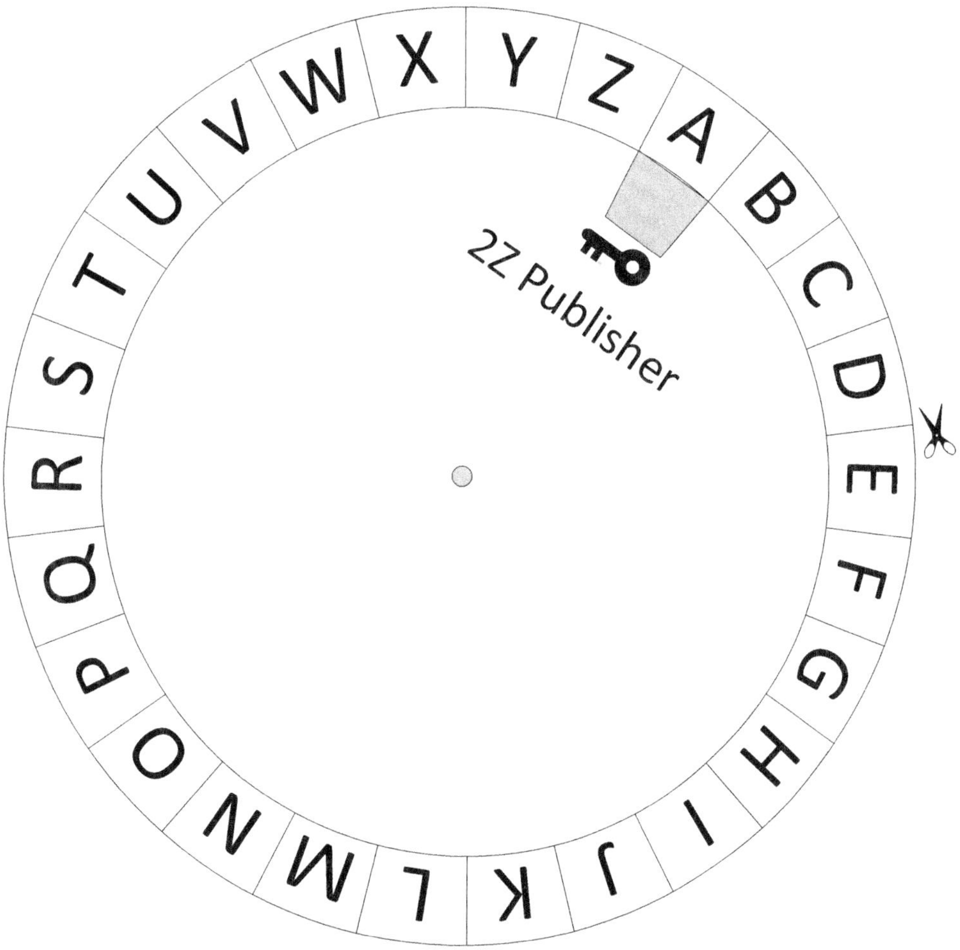

Template.2 (Small circle)

MORSE CODE

Learn and practice Morse code in a different way by using your phone

Scan QR code to learn and practice Morse Code

"The secret of getting ahead is getting started"
– Mark Twain

Date / /

A	B	C	D	E	F	G	H	I	J	K	L	M
.-	-...	-.-.	-..	.	..-.	--.	....	..	.---	-.-	.-..	--

N	O	P	Q	R	S	T	U	V	W	X	Y	Z
-.	---	.--.	--.-	.-.	...	-	..-	...-	.--	-..-	-.--	--..

Date / /

A	B	C	D	E	F	G	H	I	J	K	L	M
•▬	▬•••	▬•▬•	▬••	•	••▬•	▬▬•	••••	••	•▬▬▬	▬•▬	•▬••	▬▬
N	O	P	Q	R	S	T	U	V	W	X	Y	Z
▬•	▬▬▬	•▬▬•	▬▬•▬	•▬•	•••	▬	••▬	•••▬	•▬▬	▬••▬	▬•▬▬	▬▬••

Date / /

A	B	C	D	E	F	G	H	I	J	K	L	M
• ▬	▬ • • •	▬ • ▬ •	▬ • •	•	• • ▬ •	▬ ▬ •	• • • •	• •	• ▬ ▬ ▬	▬ • ▬	• ▬ • •	▬ ▬
N	O	P	Q	R	S	T	U	V	W	X	Y	Z
▬ •	▬ ▬ ▬	• ▬ ▬ •	▬ ▬ • ▬	• ▬ •	• • •	▬	• • ▬	• • • ▬	• ▬ ▬	▬ • • ▬	▬ • ▬ ▬	▬ ▬ • •

Date / /

A	B	C	D	E	F	G	H	I	J	K	L	M
•—	—•••	—•—•	—••	•	••—•	——•	••••	••	•———	—•—	•—••	——

N	O	P	Q	R	S	T	U	V	W	X	Y	Z
—•	———	•——•	——•—	•—•	•••	—	••—	•••—	•——	—••—	—•——	——••

1	2	3	4	5
.----	..---	...--	....-	.....
6	7	8	9	0
-....	--...	---..	----.	-----
(		@		)
-.--.		.--.-.		-.--.-
.	?	!	'	,
.-.-.-	..--..	-.-.--	.----.	--..--
+	-	/	=	:
.-.-.	-....-	-..-.	-...-	---...

1 .----

Match Letters to Morse Code

1 1	☐ .----
2 9	☐ .- ---
3 AO	☐ . .. ..
4 EII	☐ ----.

Writing Practice

1 .---- 19 .---- ----.

1 .---- 19 .---- ----.

Read Aloud

1 di dah dah dah dah

1 di dah dah dah dah

1 di dah dah dah dah

1 di dah dah dah dah

1 di dah dah dah dah

Extract the Number "1" and circle it:-(6)

.---- ----. .---- ----. .----

.---- ..--- ...-- ....-

----- .---- .---- ..--- -....

Learned

0 1 2 3 4 5 6 7 8 9

----- .---- ..--- ...-- ....- ..... -.... --... ---.. ----.

2 ..---

Match Letters to Morse Code

1 2	☐ .. ---
2 8	☐ ..---
3 IO	☐ ---..
4 IMT	☐ .. -- -

Writing Practice

2 ..---   28 ..--- ---..

2 ..---   28 ..--- ---..

Read Aloud

2 di di dah dah dah

2 di di dah dah dah

2 di di dah dah dah

2 di di dah dah dah

2 di di dah dah dah

Extract the Number "2" and circle it:-(4)

..--- ---.. ..--- ---.. ..---

.---- ..--- ...-- ....- .....

....- -.... ...-- .....

Learned

0 ----- 1 .---- 2 ..--- 3 ...-- 4 ....- 5 ..... 6 -.... 7 --... 8 ---.. 9 ----.

3 •••▬ ▬

Match Letters to Morse Code

1	3	☐	.. .- -
2	7	☐	--...
3	SM	☐	...--
4	IAT	☐	... --

Writing Practice

3 •••▬ ▬   37 ...-- --...

3 •••▬ ▬   37 ...-- --...

Read Aloud

3 di di di dah dah

3 di di di dah dah

3 di di di dah dah

3 di di di dah dah

3 di di di dah dah

Extract the Number "3" and circle it:-(3)

.---- ..--- ...-- ....-

....- ..... -.... --...

...-- ---.. --... --... ...--

Learned 0 1 2 3 4 5 6 7 8 9

.---- ..--- ...--

4 ....-

Match Letters to Morse Code

1 4	☐ -....
2 6	☐ .. .. -
3 HT	☐ .... -
4 IIT	☐ ....-

Writing Practice

4 ....- 46 ....- -....

4 ....- 46 ....- -....

Read Aloud

4 di di di di dah

4 di di di di dah

4 di di di di dah

4 di di di di dah

4 di di di di dah

Extract the Number "4" and circle it:-(2)

-.... .---- ..--- ...-- ....-

....- ..... -.... --...

---.. ----. -----

Learned

0 -----
1 .----
2 ..---
3 ...--
4 ....-
5 .....
6 -....
7 --...
8 ---..
9 ----.

5 •••••

Match Letters to Morse Code

1 5	☐ .... .
2 0	☐ -----
3 HE	☐ .. .. .
4 IIE	☐ .....

Writing Practice

5 ••••• 50 ..... -----

5 ••••• 50 ..... -----

Read Aloud

5 di di di di dit

5 di di di di dit

5 di di di di dit

5 di di di di dit

5 di di di di dit

Extract the Number "5" and circle it:-(3)

.---- ..--- ...-- ....- .....

..... -.... --... ---.. ----.

----. ...-- ...-- ....---

○Learned

0 ----- 1 .---- 2 ..--- 3 ...-- 4 ....- 5 ..... 6 -.... 7 --... 8 ---.. 9 ----.

6 -....

Match Letters to Morse Code

1 6	☐ -....
2 4	☐ ....-
3 TH	☐ -....
4 NEI	☐ -. . ..

Writing Practice

6 -.... 64 ....- -....

6 -.... 64 ....- -....

Read Aloud

6 dah di di di dit

6 dah di di di dit

6 dah di di di dit

6 dah di di di dit

6 dah di di di dit

Extract the Number "6" and circle it:-(3)

....- ..... -.... ....- -----

---.. --... ....- ....- .----

-.... ...-- ..--- ....- -....

Learned

0	1	2	3	4	5	6	7	8	9
-----	.----	..---	...--	....-	.....	-....	--...	---..	----.

7 ▬ ▬ ● ● ●

Match Letters to Morse Code

1 7	☐ -....
2 3	☐ ....-
3 TH	☐ -....
4 NEI	☐ -. . ..

Writing Practice

7 --...   73 --... ...--

Read Aloud

7 dah dah di di dit

7 dah dah di di dit

7 dah dah di di dit

7 dah dah di di dit

7 dah dah di di dit

Extract the Number "7" and circle it:-(2)

....- ..... -.... --... ---..

--... .---- .---- ....- ...--

-.... ...-- ..--- ....-

Learned

0 ----- 1 .---- 2 ..--- 3 ...-- 4 ....- 5 ..... 6 -.... 7 --... 8 ---.. 9 ----.

8 ---..

Match Letters to Morse Code

1	8	☐	---..
2	2	☐	..---
3	OI	☐	-- - ..
4	MTI	☐	--- ..

Writing Practice

8 ---.. 82 ---.. ..---

8 ---.. 82 ---.. ..---

Read Aloud

8 dah dah dah di dit

8 dah dah dah di dit

8 dah dah dah di dit

8 dah dah dah di dit

8 dah dah dah di dit

Extract the Number "8" and circle it:-(3)

.---- ..--- ...-- ..--- ---..

..... ---.. ....- -.... ---..

..--- ...-- .---- ----. ....-

Learned

0 ----- 1 .---- 2 ..--- 3 ...-- 4 ....- 5 ..... 6 -.... 7 --... 8 ---.. 9 ----.

9 ----.

Match Letters to Morse Code

1 9	☐ .----
2 1	☐ .. .. .
3 IIE	☐ --- .-
4 OA	☐ ----.

Writing Practice

9 ----. 91 .---- ----.

9 ----. 91 .---- ----.

Read Aloud

9 dah dah dah dah dit

9 dah dah dah dah dit

9 dah dah dah dah dit

9 dah dah dah dah dit

9 dah dah dah dah dit

Extract the Number "9" and circle it:-(4)

.---- ----. .---- ----.

.---- ----. ----.

.---- ..--- -.... ....- .....

Learned

0	1	2	3	4	5	6	7	8	9
-----	.----	..---	...--	....-	.....	-....	--...	---..	----.

0 -----

Match Letters to Morse Code

1 0	☐ -- ---
2 5	☐ -----
3 MO	☐ -- -- -
4 MMT	☐ .....

Writing Practice

0 ----- 05 ----- .....

0 ----- 05 ----- .....

Read Aloud

0 dah dah dah dah dah

0 dah dah dah dah dah

0 dah dah dah dah dah

0 dah dah dah dah dah

0 dah dah dah dah dah

Extract the Number "0" and circle it:-(4)

----- .---- ..--- ...-- ....-

...-- ..--- ..... ----- ..---

....- ----- .---- ...-- -----

⊘Learned

0	1	2	3	4	5	6	7	8	9
-----	.----	..---	...--	....-	.....	-....	--...	---..	----.

Date / /

0 1 2 3 4 5 6 7 8 9

Date / /

0 1 2 3 4 5 6 7 8 9

−−−−− ·−−−− ··−−− ···−− ····− ····· −···· −−··· −−−·· −−−−·

Date / /

0 1 2 3 4 5 6 7 8 9

Date / /

0 1 2 3 4 5 6 7 8 9

ACTIVITY FOR KIDS

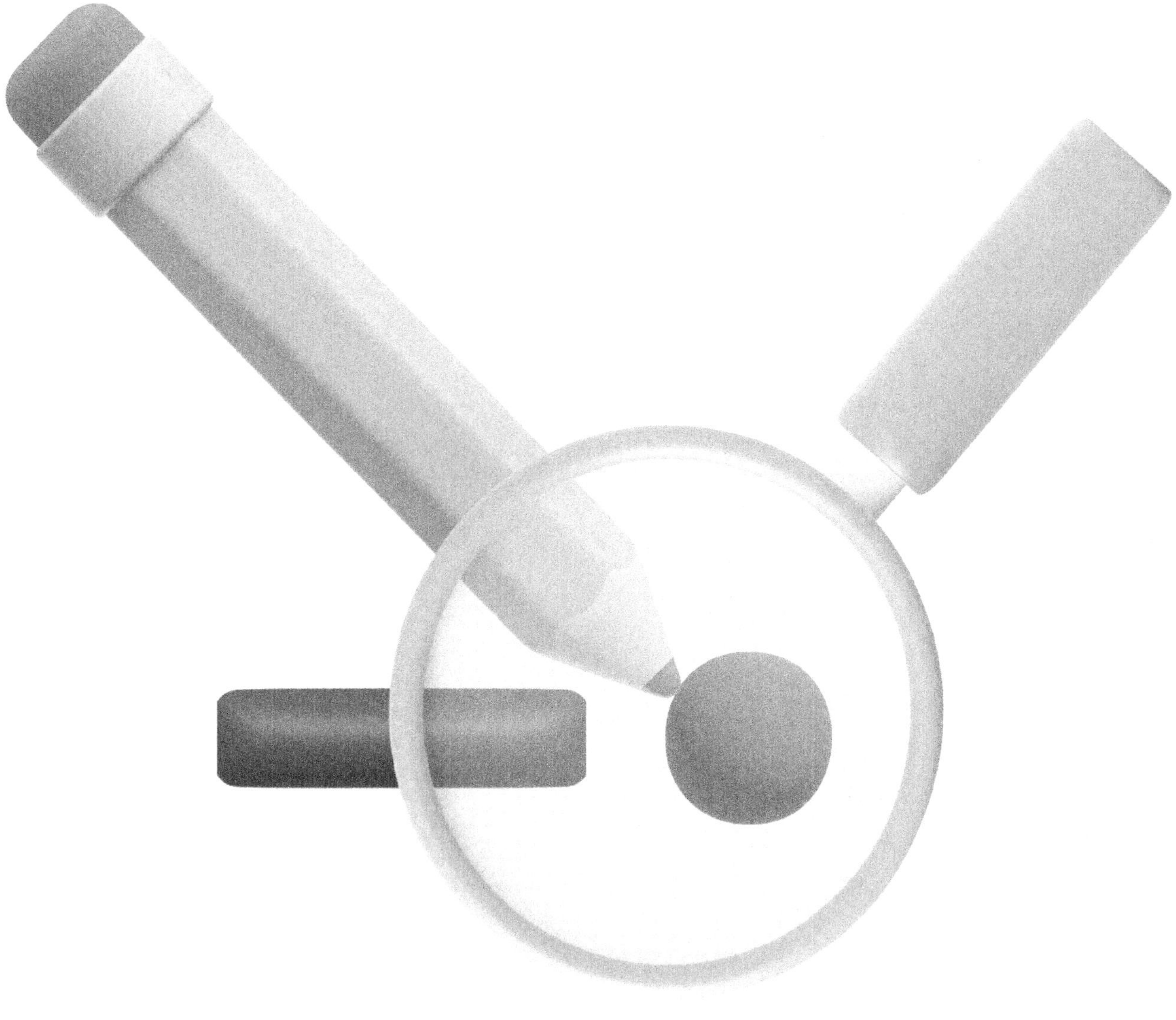

CIPHER WHEEL

With Numbers

Make a cipher wheel and use it to send secret messages to your friends and family.

Replace the smaller letter circle with the number circle. Now you can encrypt messages with numbers instead of letters.

This activity involves making a cipher wheel and using it to encrypt and decrypt messages with your friend or with your family, with a simple cipher made of paper.

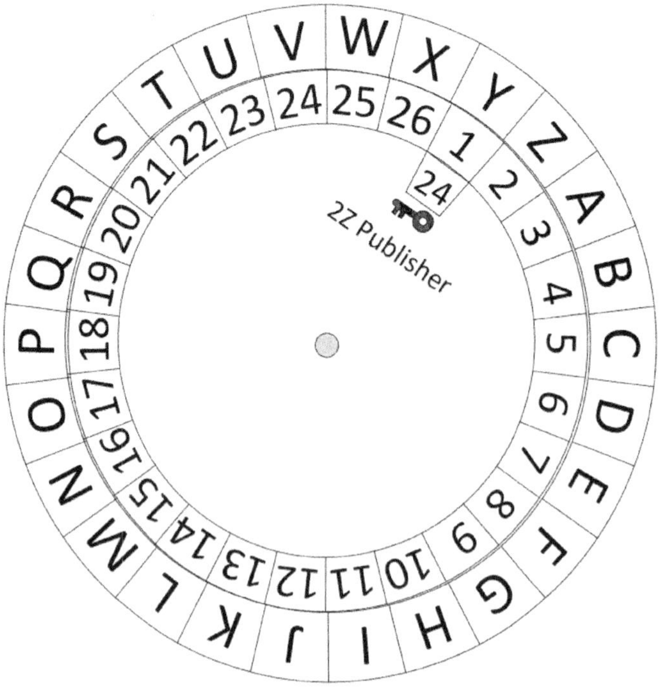

What this activity is?

Using the cipher wheel to encrypt a message -make it secret- involves transforming each letter of the message into a number by following a series of steps:

In this case, encrypting a message involves simply shifting each letter of the message by a certain number of places through the alphabet.

The message's receiver is aware of the encryption key– which, in the case of cryptography, is called a cipher – and can decrypt the messages by applying the process in reverse (decoding the secret message).

Needed Tools:

1. Pencil for making notes and writing messages.
2. Split Pin Paper Fasteners
   (Paper fasteners can be replaced by blue tack and wooden skewer).
3. Card Stock circles with the same size of templates
   (To make the cipher wheel rigid and last longer).
4. Glue (To stick the wheel to the Card stock).
5. Plastic Scissors.
6. Cipher Wheel templates (Numbers template).

   2 Copies are included for free in this book for our little heroes.

Follow these steps...

1. Cut the templates with the help of your parents.
2. Cut the card stock circles with the help of your parents.
3. Glue the Cipher wheel templates to the card stock circles.
4. Put the small circle on the large circle and secure it with a split pin in the center.
5. Choose a "key" or "shift", The number of letters the alphabet will be shifted by.
   E.g. with a shift of **24** A becomes **3**.
6. Rotate the front disc until the chosen shift is set. The shift number will appear in the "Key" window so that each number on smaller Wheel lines up with a letter on the larger wheel.
7. Now encrypt your message (make it secret).
   For each letter, write down the number on the smaller wheel that appears directly beneath it.
8. Don't forget to record your secret key. Either as the shift number as A=3 for Key=**24** as you will need it to decode your secret message.
9. Encrypt messages to a friend in letters, and ask them to send you encrypted messages too, and their secret keys.
10. For example, "SECRET" and for(Key = **24**) word will be "21.7.5.20.7.22" = "SECRET".
11. There is an additional copy of these templates in the last papers of this book so you can gift it to your loved friends or to family members to play together and enjoy this activity.

12. Scan QR Code for more understanding

(YouTube playlist that contains **2** Videos)

Try to encrypt next messages:

- I enjoy learning Morse code.
- Keep our secret.
- I love my family.
- Hello my friend.
- The enemy base is in the north.

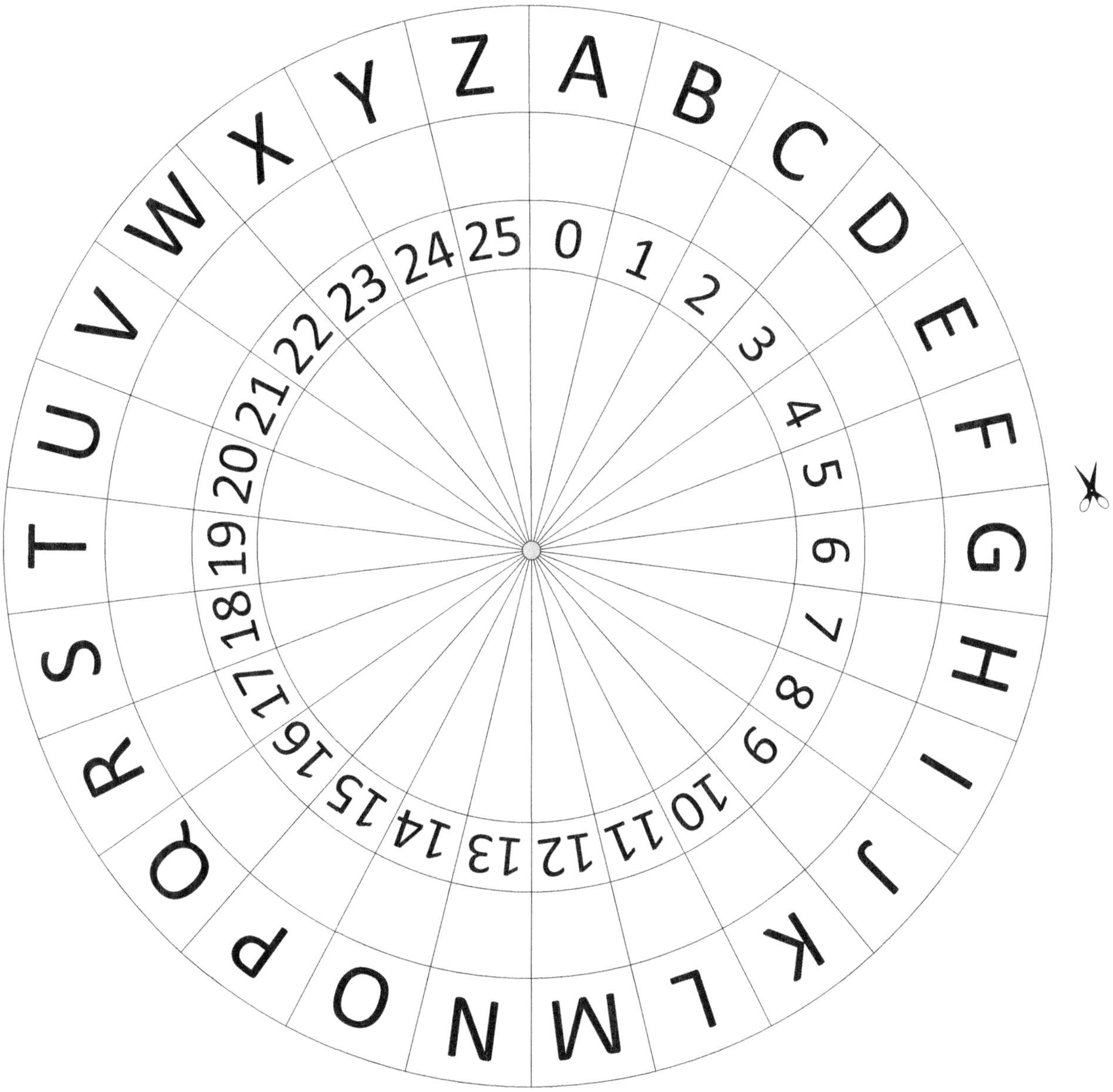

Template.1 (Large circle)

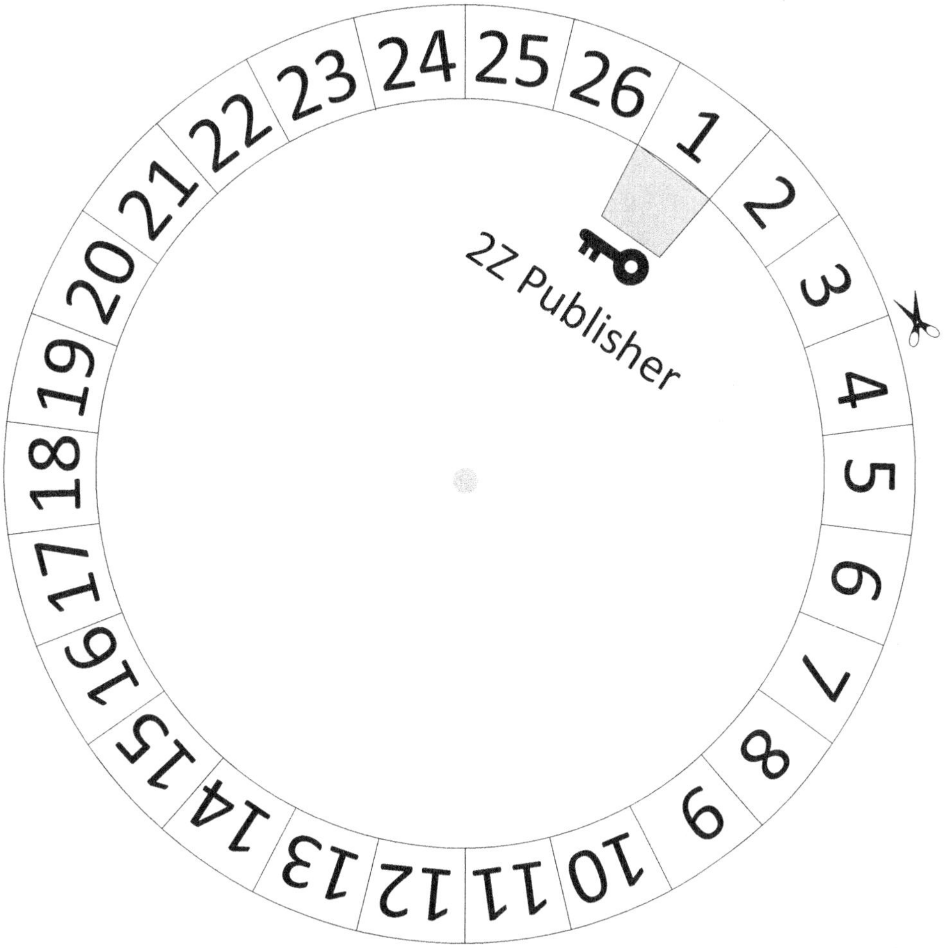

Template.2 (Small circle)

PRACTICE FOR KIDS

A	B	C	D	E	F	G	H	I
•–	–•••	–•–•	–••	•	••–•	––•	••••	••

J	K	L	M	N	O	P	Q	R
•–––	–•–	•–••	––	–•	–––	•––•	––•–	•–•

S	T	U	V	W	X	Y	Z
•••	–	••–	•••–	•––	–••–	–•––	––••

1	2	3	4	5
·−−−−	··−−−	···−−	····−	·····
6	7	8	9	0
−····	−−···	−−−··	−−−−·	−−−−−
(		@		)
−·−−·		·−−·−·		−·−−·−
.	?	!	'	,
·−·−·−	··−−··	−·−·−−	·−−−−·	−−··−−
+	-	/	=	:
·−·−·	−····−	−··−·	−···−	−−−···

Translate text to Morse code

Take it easy

- .- -.- . / .. - / . .- ... -.-- — Translation

I am good

A	B	C	D	E	F	G	H	I	J	K	L	M
.-	-...	-.-.	-..	.	..-.	--.	....	..	.---	-.-	.-..	--
N	**O**	**P**	**Q**	**R**	**S**	**T**	**U**	**V**	**W**	**X**	**Y**	**Z**
-.	---	.--.	--.-	.-.	...	-	..-	...-	.--	-..-	-.--	--..

Translate text to Morse code

How are you

How you doing

A	B	C	D	E	F	G	H	I	J	K	L	M
•—	—•••	—•—•	—••	•	••—•	——•	••••	••	•———	—•—	•—••	——

N	O	P	Q	R	S	T	U	V	W	X	Y	Z
—•	———	•——•	——•—	•—•	•••	—	••—	•••—	•——	—••—	—•——	——••

Translate text to Morse code

Would you mind closing the door

How much does this cost

A	B	C	D	E	F	G	H	I	J	K	L	M
•—	—•••	—•—•	—••	•	••—•	——•	••••	••	•———	—•—	•—••	——
N	**O**	**P**	**Q**	**R**	**S**	**T**	**U**	**V**	**W**	**X**	**Y**	**Z**
—•	———	•——•	——•—	•—•	•••	—	••—	•••—	•——	—••—	—•——	——••

Translate text to Morse code

I live close to my family

I brush my teeth every day

A	B	C	D	E	F	G	H	I	J	K	L	M
•—	—•••	—•—•	—••	•	••—•	——•	••••	••	•———	—•—	•—••	——
N	O	P	Q	R	S	T	U	V	W	X	Y	Z
—•	———	•——•	——•—	•—•	•••	—	••—	•••—	•——	—••—	—•——	——••

Translate text to Morse code

I am learning Morse Code

I am reading a book

A	B	C	D	E	F	G	H	I	J	K	L	M
.-	-...	-.-.	-..	.	..-.	--.	....	..	.---	-.-	.-..	--
N	O	P	Q	R	S	T	U	V	W	X	Y	Z
-.	---	.--.	--.-	.-.	...	-	..-	...-	.--	-..-	-.--	--..

Translate text to Morse code

Save our souls SOS

SOS

Help

A	B	C	D	E	F	G	H	I	J	K	L	M
•–	–•••	–•–•	–••	•	••–•	––•	••••	••	•–––	–•–	•–••	––

N	O	P	Q	R	S	T	U	V	W	X	Y	Z
–•	–––	•––•	––•–	•–•	•••	–	••–	•••–	•––	–••–	–•––	––••

Decode Morse code to text

--. --- --- -.. / .- ..-. - . .-. -. --- --- -.

Good Afternoon — Decoding

.... --- .-- / .- .-. . / -.-- --- ..- / -.. --- .. -. --.

A	B	C	D	E	F	G	H	I	J	K	L	M
.-	-...	-.-.	-..	.	..-.	--.	....	..	.---	-.-	.-..	--
N	O	P	Q	R	S	T	U	V	W	X	Y	Z
-.	---	.--.	--.-	.-.	...	-	..-	...-	.--	-..-	-.--	--..

Decode Morse code to text

.. / .-- .- -.- . / ..- .--. / .- - / --... .- --

A	B	C	D	E	F	G	H	I	J	K	L	M
.-	-...	-.-.	-..	.	..-.	--.	....	..	.---	-.-	.-..	--

N	O	P	Q	R	S	T	U	V	W	X	Y	Z
-.	---	.--.	--.-	.-.	...	-	..-	...-	.--	-..-	-.--	--..

Decode Morse code to text

.. / --. --- / - --- / .-- --- .-. -.- /

. ...- . .-. -.-- / -.. .- -.--

A	B	C	D	E	F	G	H	I	J	K	L	M
.-	-...	-.-.	-..	.	..-.	--.	....	..	.---	-.-	.-..	--

N	O	P	Q	R	S	T	U	V	W	X	Y	Z
-.	---	.--.	--.-	.-.	...	-	..-	...-	.--	-..-	-.--	--..

Decode Morse code to text

.. / .- -- / --. --- .. -. --. / - --- /

--. . - / -- .- .-. .-. .. . -.. / .. -. /

.- / ..-. . .-- / -.-- . .- .-. ...

A	B	C	D	E	F	G	H	I	J	K	L	M
.-	-...	-.-.	-..	.	..-.	--.	....	..	.---	-.-	.-..	--
N	O	P	Q	R	S	T	U	V	W	X	Y	Z
-.	---	.--.	--.-	.-.	...	-	..-	...-	.--	-..-	-.--	--..

Decode Morse code to text

.. / .-.. .. -.- . / - --- / ... .--. . -. -.. / - .. -- . /

.-- .. - .... / -- -.-- / ..-. .- -- .. .-.. -.-- / .- -. -.. /

..-. .-. .. . -. -.. ... / .. -. / -- -.-- / ..-. .-. . . /

- .. -- .

A	B	C	D	E	F	G	H	I	J	K	L	M
.-	-...	-.-.	-..	.	..-.	--.	....	..	.---	-.-	.-..	--
N	**O**	**P**	**Q**	**R**	**S**	**T**	**U**	**V**	**W**	**X**	**Y**	**Z**
-.	---	.--.	--.-	.-.	...	-	..-	...-	.--	-..-	-.--	--..

Decode Morse code to text

.... --- .-- / .- .-. . / -.-- --- ..- / -.. --- .. -. --.

A	B	C	D	E	F	G	H	I	J	K	L	M
.-	-...	-.-.	-..	.	..-.	--.	....	..	.---	-.-	.-..	--

N	O	P	Q	R	S	T	U	V	W	X	Y	Z
-.	---	.--.	--.-	.-.	...	-	..-	...-	.--	-..-	-.--	--..

Decode Morse code to text

.... --- .-- / .- .-. . / -.-- --- ..- / -.. --- .. -. --. .. /

.-.. --- --- -.- / ..-. --- .-. .-- .- .-. -.. / - --- /

... . -. --. / -.-- --- ..- / .- --. .- .. -.

A	B	C	D	E	F	G	H	I	J	K	L	M
.-	-...	-.-.	-..	.	..-.	--.	....	..	.---	-.-	.-..	--

N	O	P	Q	R	S	T	U	V	W	X	Y	Z
-.	---	.--.	--.-	.-.	...	-	..-	...-	.--	-..-	-.--	--..

Decode Morse code to text

..--- --.. / .--. ..- -... .-.. .. ..-.

A	B	C	D	E	F	G	H	I	J	K	L	M
.-	-...	-.-.	-..	.	..-.	--.	....	..	.---	-.-	.-..	--

N	O	P	Q	R	S	T	U	V	W	X	Y	Z
-.	---	.--.	--.-	.-.	...	-	..-	...-	.--	-..-	-.--	--..

Decode Morse code to text

• • • — — — • • •

• • • • • • — • • • — — •

A	B	C	D	E	F	G	H	I	J	K	L	M
• —	— • • •	— • — •	— • •	•	• • — •	— — •	• • • •	• •	• — — —	— • —	• — • •	— —
N	**O**	**P**	**Q**	**R**	**S**	**T**	**U**	**V**	**W**	**X**	**Y**	**Z**
— •	— — —	• — — •	— — • —	• — •	• • •	—	• • —	• • • —	• — —	— • • —	— • — —	— — • •

Date / /

1	2	3	4	5
.----	..---	...--	....-	.....
6	7	8	9	0
-....	--...	---..	----.	-----
(		@		)
-.--.		.--.-.		-.--.-
.	?	!	'	,
.-.-.-	..--..	-.-.--	.----.	--..--
+	-	/	=	:
.-.-.	-....-	-..-.	-...-	---...

= -...-

Match Letters to Morse Code

1 =	☐ -.. .-
2 DA	☐ -...-
3 TST	☐ -. . . -
4 NEET	☐ - ... -

Writing Practice

=	-...-	=5	-...- .....
=	-...-	=5	-...- .....

Read Aloud

= dah di di di dah

= dah di di di dah

= dah di di di dah

= dah di di di dah

= dah di di di dah

Extract the Symbol "=" and circle it:-(1)

-.. .- / ...-- ..--- ....--

-...- ...-- ..--- ....--

/ -.. .- /

Learned = -...- - + . / : ? ! ' ,

Match Letters to Morse Code

1 -	☐ -.. ..-
2 DU	☐ -....-
3 THT	☐ -. .. . -
4 NIET	☐ - .... -

Writing Practice

- -....-	-= -....- -...-
- -....-	-= -....- -...-

Read Aloud

- dah di di di di dah

- dah di di di di dah

- dah di di di di dah

- dah di di di di dah

- dah di di di di dah

Extract the Symbol "-" and circle it:-(1)

..... -....- ...-- -...- ..---

-...- ...-- ..--- ....--

/ -.. .- /

Learned = -...- - -....- + . / : ? ! ' ,

+ .-.-.	**Match Letters to Morse Code**

Match Letters to Morse Code

1	+	☐	.-. -.
2	RN	☐	. - .-.
3	RTE	☐	.-. - .
4	ETR	☐	.-.-.

Writing Practice

+ .-.-. +- .-.-. -....-

Read Aloud

+ di dah di dah dit

+ di dah di dah dit

+ di dah di dah dit

+ di dah di dah dit

+ di dah di dah dit

Extract the Symbol "+" and circle it:-(2)

..... -....- ...-- -...- ---..

..... .-.-. ...-- -...- ---..

.---- ..--- ...-- / .-.-.

Learned

= -...-   - -....-   + .-.-.

.   .-.-.-

Match Letters to Morse Code

1 .	☐ .-. -.-
2 RK	☐ .-. - .-
3 RTA	☐ .-.-.-
4 ETAA	☐ . - .- .-

Writing Practice

. .-.-.-   .+ .-.-.- .-.-.

. .-.-.-   .+ .-.-.- .-.-.

Read Aloud

. di dah di dah di dah

. di dah di dah di dah

. di dah di dah di dah

. di dah di dah di dah

. di dah di dah di dah

Extract the Symbol "." and circle it:-(2)

..... -....- ...-- -...- ---..

..... .-.-. .-.-.- -...- ---..

.-.-.- ..--- ...-- / .-.-.

Learned

= -...-   - -....-   + .-.-.   . .-.-.-   / -..-.   : ---...   ? ..--..   ! -.-.--   ’ .----.   , --..--

/ -..-.

Match Letters to Morse Code

1 /	☐ -..-.
2 NR	☐ -. . -.
3 NEN	☐ -. .-.
4 TITE	☐ - .. - .

Writing Practice

/ -..-.   /.   -..-. .-.-.-

Read Aloud

/ dah di di dah dit

/ dah di di dah dit

/ dah di di dah dit

/ dah di di dah dit

/ dah di di dah dit

Extract the Symbol "/" and circle it:-(1)

..... -....- ...-- -...- ---..

.---- ----- -..-. ..... -...-

..--- / .---- ..--- ...-- / .-.-.

Learned

= -...-   - -....-   + .-.-.   . .-.-.-   / -..-.   : ---...   ? ..--..   ! -.-.--   ' .----.   , --..--

:

---...

Match Letters to Morse Code

1 :	☐ ---...
2 OS	☐ --- ...
3 MNI	☐ - -- . ..
4 TMEI	☐ -- -. ..

Writing Practice

: ---...	:/ ---... -..-.
: ---...	:/ ---... -..-.

Read Aloud

: dah dah dah di di dit

: dah dah dah di di dit

: dah dah dah di di dit

: dah dah dah di di dit

: dah dah dah di di dit

Extract the Symbol ":" and circle it:-(2)

.---- ..--- ...-- ....----

....- ---... ..... -....

.---- ..--- ...-- / ---...

Learned

= -...-   - -....-   + .-.-.   . .-.-.-   / -..-.   : ---...   ? ..--..   ! -.-.--   ' .----.   , --..--

? ..--..

Match Letters to Morse Code

1 ?	☐ .. -- ..
2 UD	☐ ..- -..
3 IMI	☐ . .- - ..
4 EATI	☐ ..--..

Writing Practice

? ..--..	?. ..--.. .-.-.-

Read Aloud

? di di dah dah di dit

? di di dah dah di dit

? di di dah dah di dit

? di di dah dah di dit

? di di dah dah di dit

Extract the Symbol "?" and circle it:-(1)

.-- .... .- - / .. ... / - .... .- -

..--.. / .-- .... .- - / .. ...

Learned

= -...-   - -....-   + .-.-.   . .-.-.-   / -..-.   : ---...   ? ..--..

! -.-.--

Match Letters to Morse Code

[1] !	[ ] - . -. --
[2] KW	[ ] -.-.--
[3] TRM	[ ] -.- .--
[4] TENM	[ ] - .-. --

Writing Practice

! -.-.--	!? -.-.-- ..--..
! -.-.--	!? -.-.-- ..--..

Read Aloud

! dah di dah di dah dah

! dah di dah di dah dah

! dah di dah di dah dah

! dah di dah di dah dah

! dah di dah di dah dah

Extract the Symbol "!" and circle it:-(1)

..--- ----- ..--- ..--- .--.-.

..--- --.. /

.--. ..- -... .-.. .. ..-.

-.-.--

Learned

= -...-   - -....-   + .-.-.   . .-.-.-   / -..-.   : ---...   ? ..--..   ! -.-.--   ' .----.   , --..--

’ .----.

Match Letters to Morse Code

[1] ’	☐ .----.
[2] WG	☐ .- -- -.
[3] AMN	☐ .- -- - .
[4] AMTE	☐ .-- --.

Writing Practice

’ .----. " .----. .----.

’ .----. " .----. .----.

Read Aloud

’ di dah dah dah dah dit

’ di dah dah dah dah dit

’ di dah dah dah dah dit

’ di dah dah dah dah dit

’ di dah dah dah dah dit

Extract the Symbol " ’ " and circle it:-(1)

..--- ----- ..--- ..--- .--.-.

..--- --.. /.----.

.--. ..- -... .-.. .. ..-.

.----.

⊘Learned = -...- - -....- + .-.-. . .-.-.- / -..-. : ---... ? ..--.. ! -.-.-- ’ .----. ’

, --..--

Match Letters to Morse Code

1 ,	☐ --. . - -
2 ZM	☐ --.. --
3 MIM	☐ -- .. --
4 GETT	☐ --..--

Writing Practice

, --..-- | , --..-- .----.

, --..-- | , --..-- .----.

Read Aloud

, dah dah di di dah dah

, dah dah di di dah dah

, dah dah di di dah dah

, dah dah di di dah dah

, dah dah di di dah dah

Extract the Symbol " , " and circle it:-(2)

..--- ----- ..--- ..--- --..--

..--- --.. / .----.

.--. ..- -... .-.. .. ..-.

--..--

⊘Learned

= -...- | - -....- | + .-.-. | . .-.-.- | / -..-. | : ---... | ? ..--.. | ! -.-.-- | ’ .----. | , --..--

(-.--.

Match Letters to Morse Code

1 (	☐ -.--.
2 KN	☐ -.- - .
3 KTE	☐ -.- -.
4 TEME	☐ - . -- .

Writing Practice

(-.--.   (= -.--. -...-

Read Aloud

(dah di dah dah dit

(dah di dah dah dit

(dah di dah dah dit

(dah di dah dah dit

(dah di dah dah dit

Extract the Symbol "(" and circle it:-(1)

-.--. .---- ..--- ...-- .....

----. ....- -....

---.. -.... ...-- .----

Learned

(-.--.   @   )

) -.--.-

Match Letters to Morse Code

1)	☐ -.--.-
2 KK	☐ -.- -.-
3 TPT	☐ - .--. -
4 TEMA	☐ - . -- .-

Writing Practice

) -.--.-)= -.--.- -...-

) -.--.-)= -.--.- -...-

Read Aloud

) dah di dah dah di dah

) dah di dah dah di dah

) dah di dah dah di dah

) dah di dah dah di dah

) dah di dah dah di dah

Extract the Symbol ")" and circle it:-(2)

-.--. - .---- ..--- ...-- .....

-.--.- ....- -....

---.. -.... ...-- -.--.-

Learned

(-.--. @ .--.-.) -.--.-

@ .--.-.

Match Letters to Morse Code

1 @	☐ .--. -.
2 PN	☐ .--.-.
3 ANN	☐ .- -. -.
4 ATEN	☐ .- - . -.

Writing Practice

@ .--.-.	@= .--.-. -...-
@ .--.-.	@= .--.-. -...-

Read Aloud

@ di dah dah di dah dit

@ di dah dah di dah dit

@ di dah dah di dah dit

@ di dah dah di dah dit

@ di dah dah di dah dit

Extract the Symbol "@" and circle it:-(1)

..--- ----- ..--- ..---

.--.-. ..--- --.. /

.--. ..- -... .-.. .. ..-.

(@)

-.--. .--.-. -.--.-

○Learned

MORSE CODE

Learn and practice Morse code in a different way by using your phone

Scan QR code to learn and practice Morse Code

"The secret of getting ahead is getting started"
– Mark Twain

ACTIVITY FOR KIDS

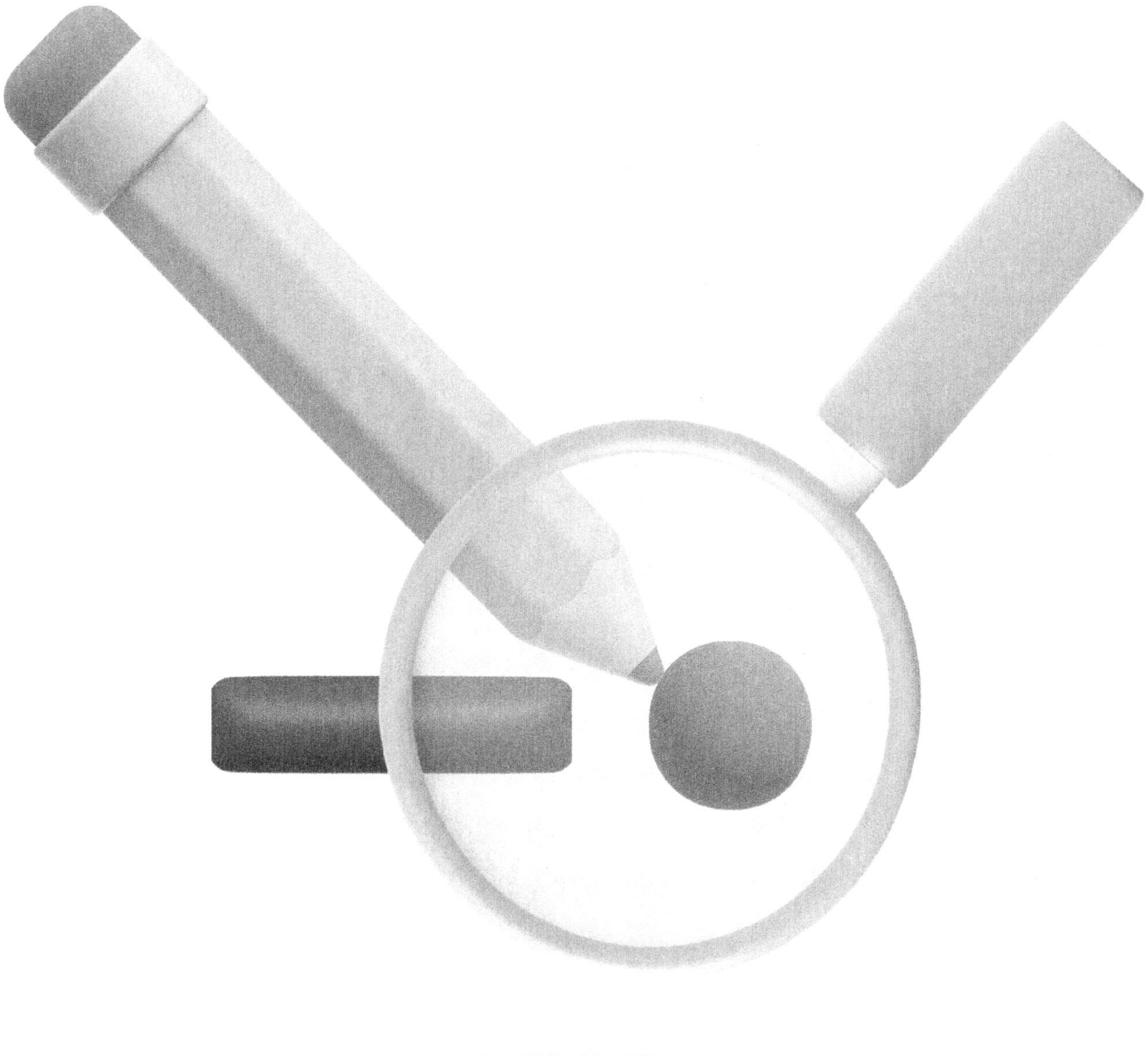

__________ WHEEL

With the help of your parents make your own secret wheel to send secret messages to your friends and family and name it as you like.

Remember: you can use Morse code letters.

This book contains 2 copies of these templates.

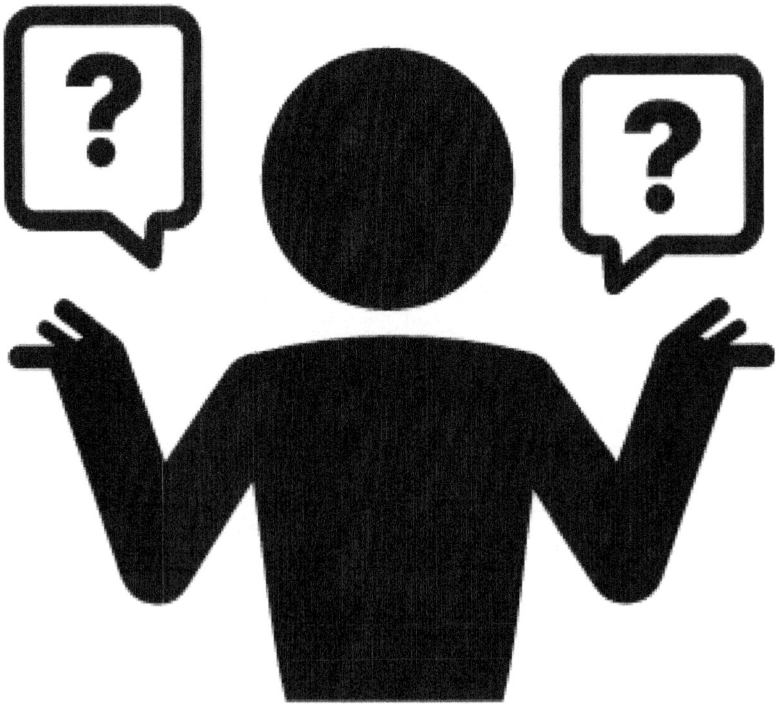

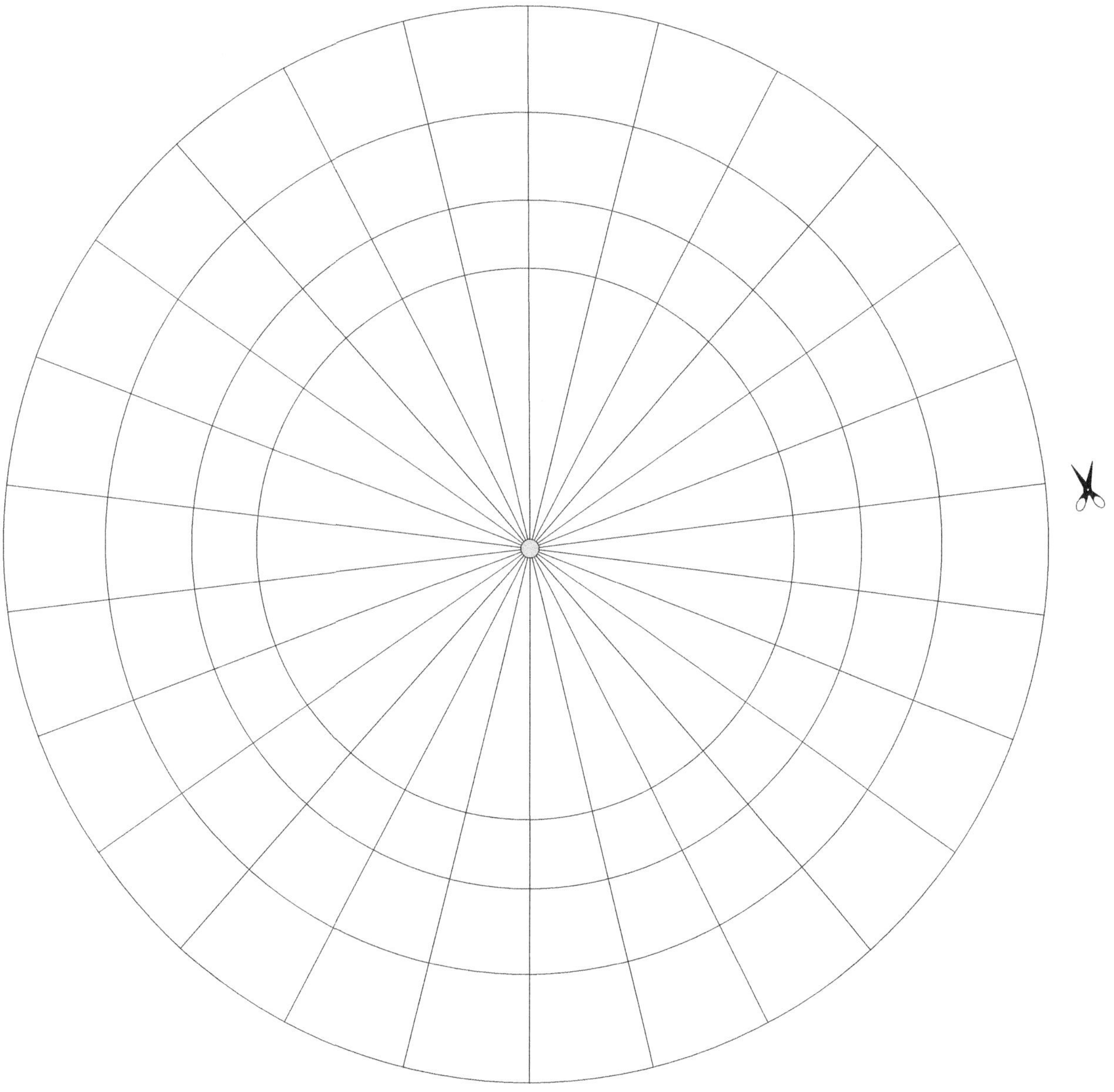

Template.1 (Large circle)
Make your own secret wheel

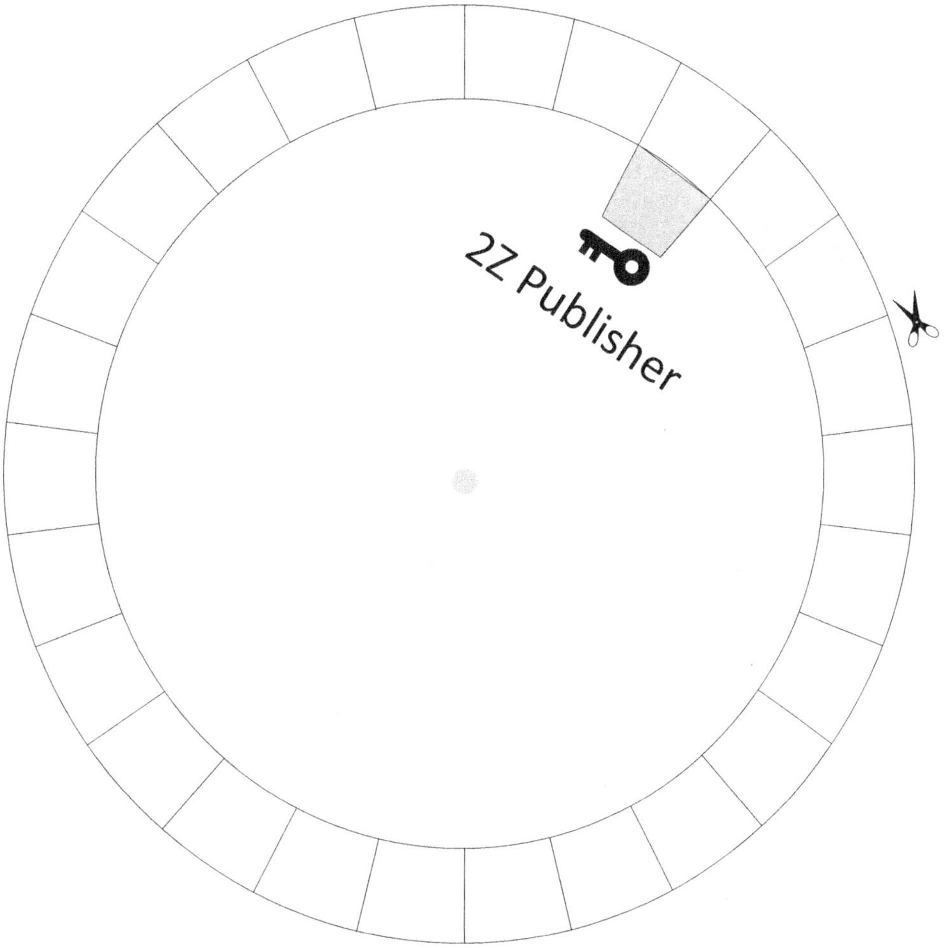

Template.2 (Small circle)
Make your own secret wheel

PRACTICE FOR KIDS

Date / /

A	B	C	D	E	F	G	H	I	J	K	L	M
•▬	▬•••	▬•▬•	▬••	•	••▬•	▬▬•	••••	••	•▬▬▬	▬•▬	•▬••	▬▬
N	O	P	Q	R	S	T	U	V	W	X	Y	Z
▬•	▬▬▬	•▬▬•	▬▬•▬	•▬•	•••	▬	••▬	•••▬	•▬▬	▬••▬	▬•▬▬	▬▬••

Date / /

0 ----- 1 .---- 2 ..--- 3 ...-- 4 ....- 5 ..... 6 -.... 7 --... 8 ---.. 9 ----.

Date / /

A	B	C	D	E	F	G	H	I	J	K	L	M
·−	−···	−·−·	−··	·	··−·	−−·	····	··	·−−−	−·−	·−··	−−

N	O	P	Q	R	S	T	U	V	W	X	Y	Z
−·	−−−	·−−·	−−·−	·−·	···	−	··−	···−	·−−	−··−	−·−−	−−··

Date / /

0 1 2 3 4 5 6 7 8 9

Date / /

A	B	C	D	E	F	G	H	I	J	K	L	M
·—	—···	—·—·	—··	·	··—·	——·	····	··	·———	—·—	·—··	——
N	O	P	Q	R	S	T	U	V	W	X	Y	Z
—·	———	·——·	——·—	·—·	···	—	··—	···—	·——	—··—	—·——	——··

Date / /

0 1 2 3 4 5 6 7 8 9

2Z Publisher's Gift for our little heroes

Free Cipher Wheels Templates

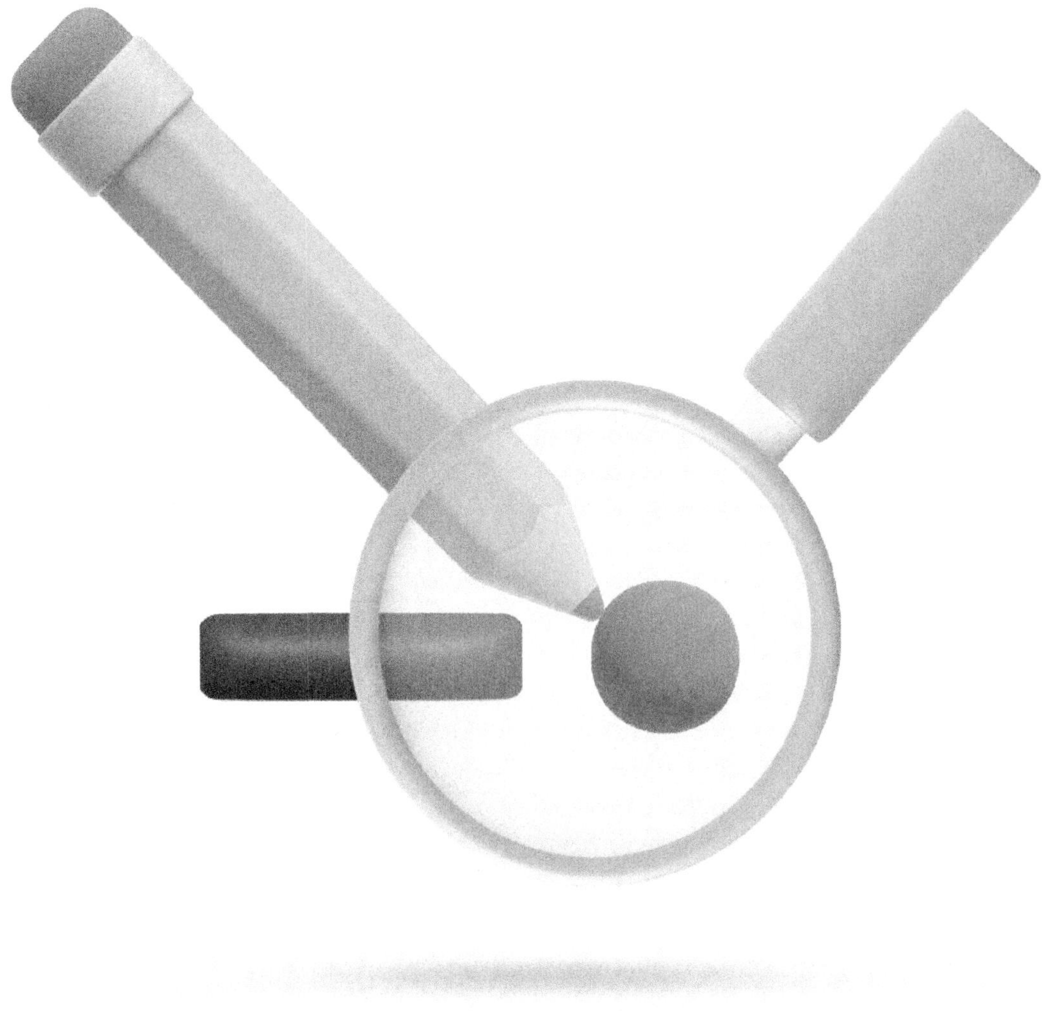

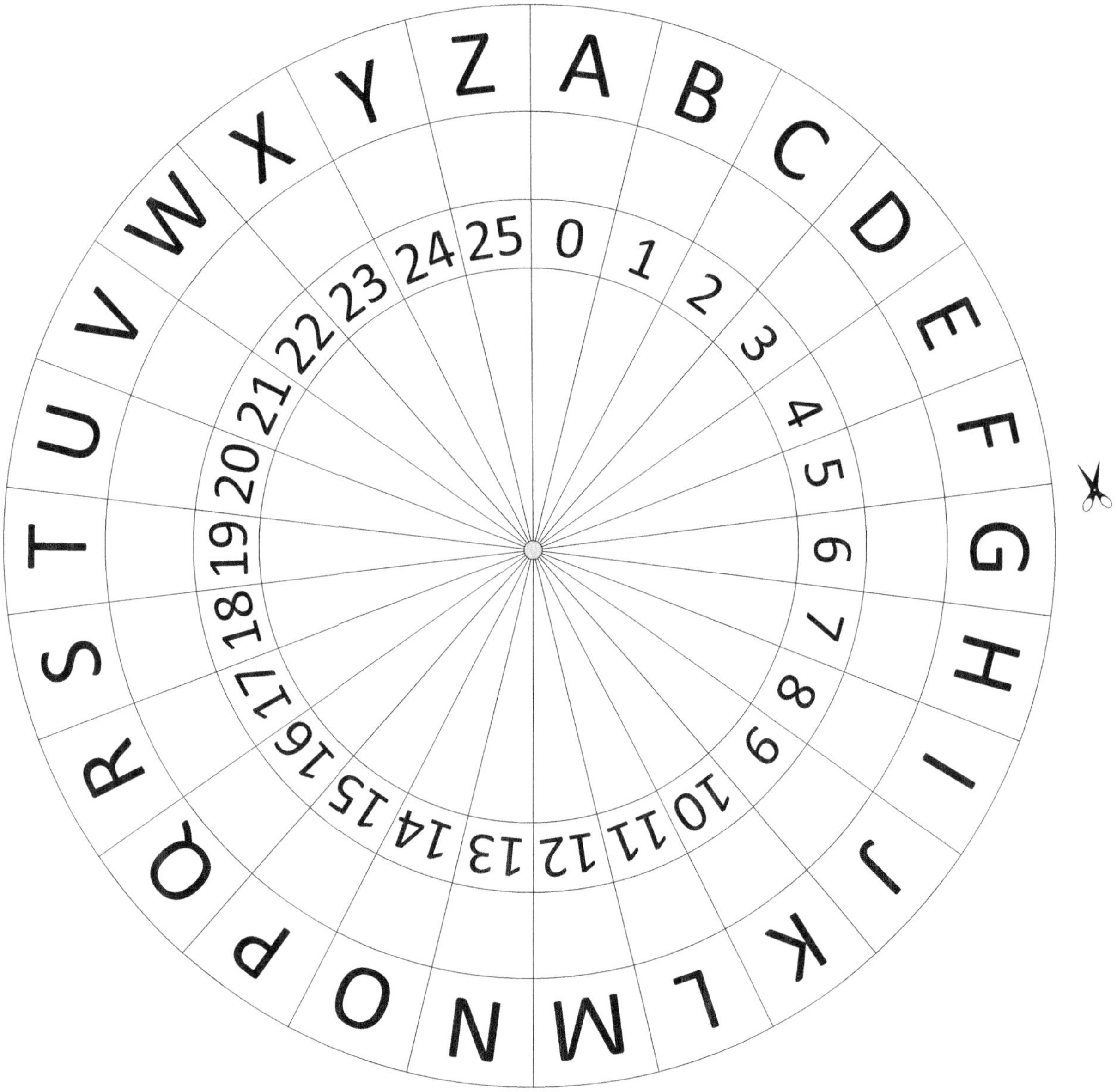

Template.1 (Large circle)

Template.2 (Small circle)

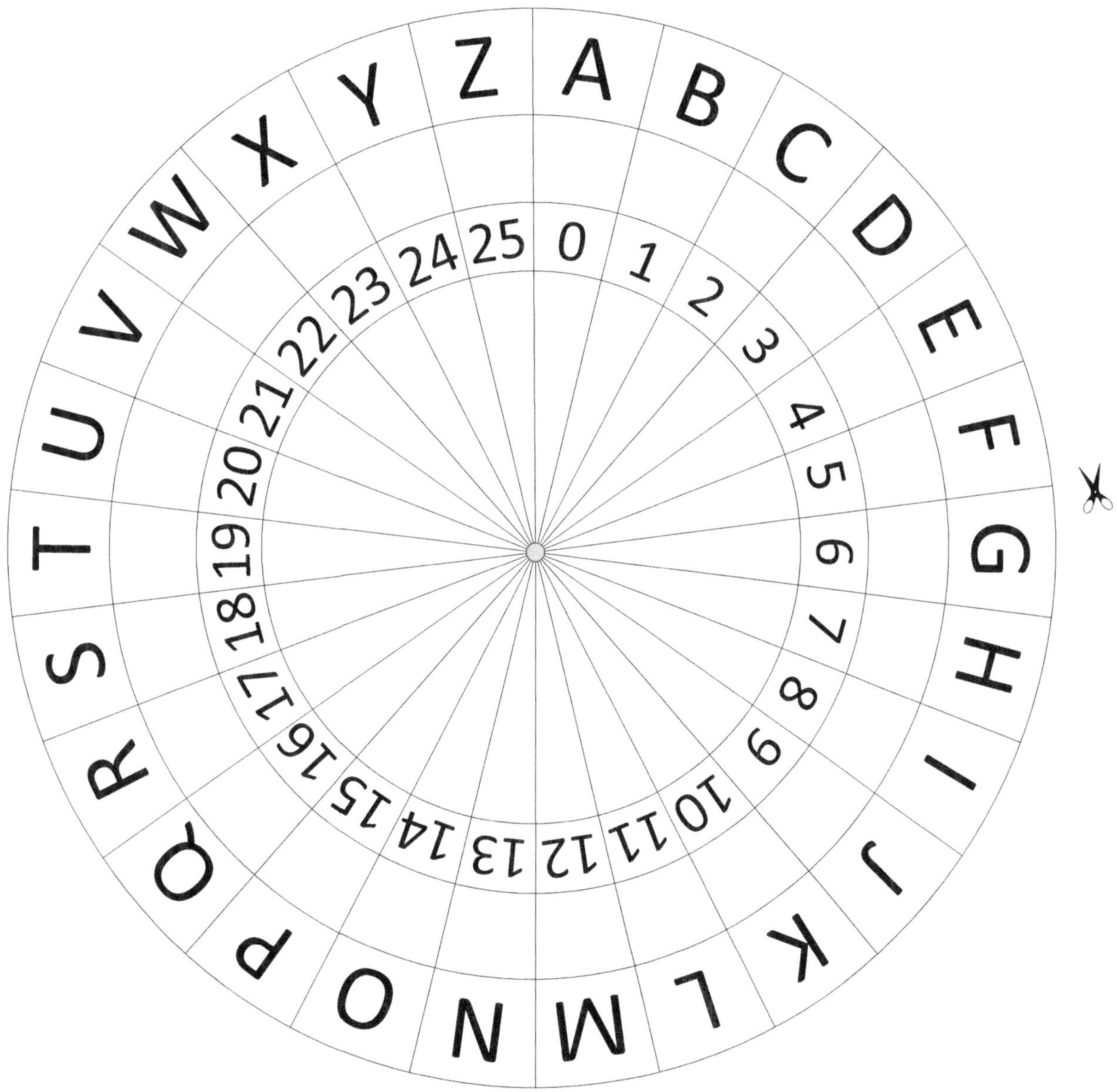

Template.1 (Large circle)

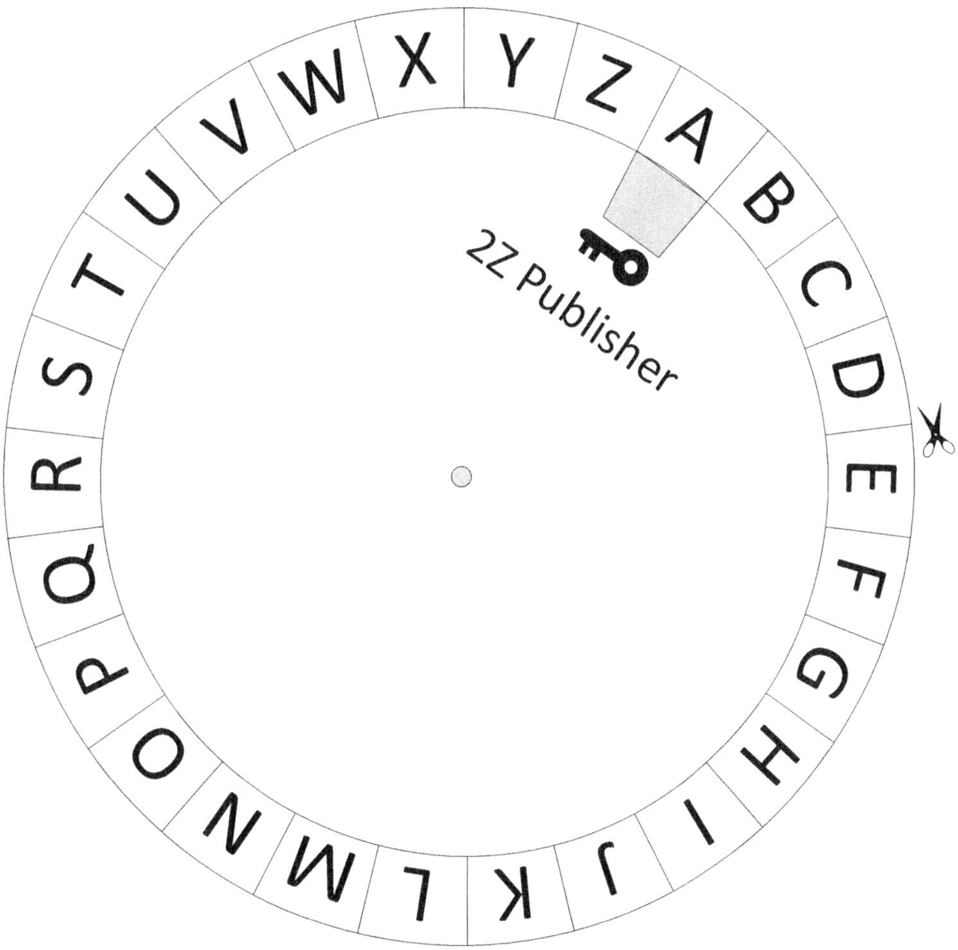

Template.2 (Small circle)

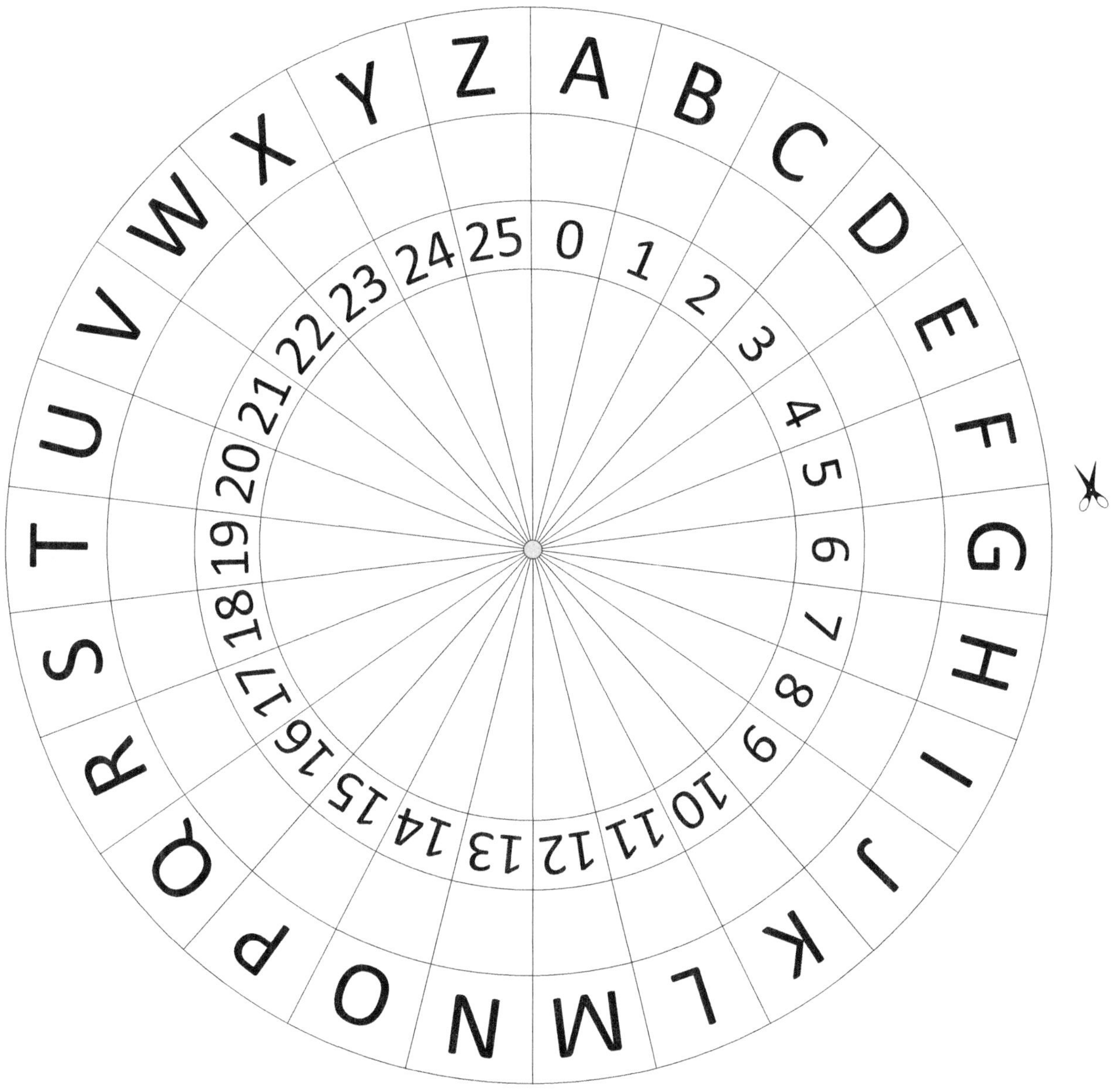

Template.1 (Large circle)

Template. 2 (Small circle)

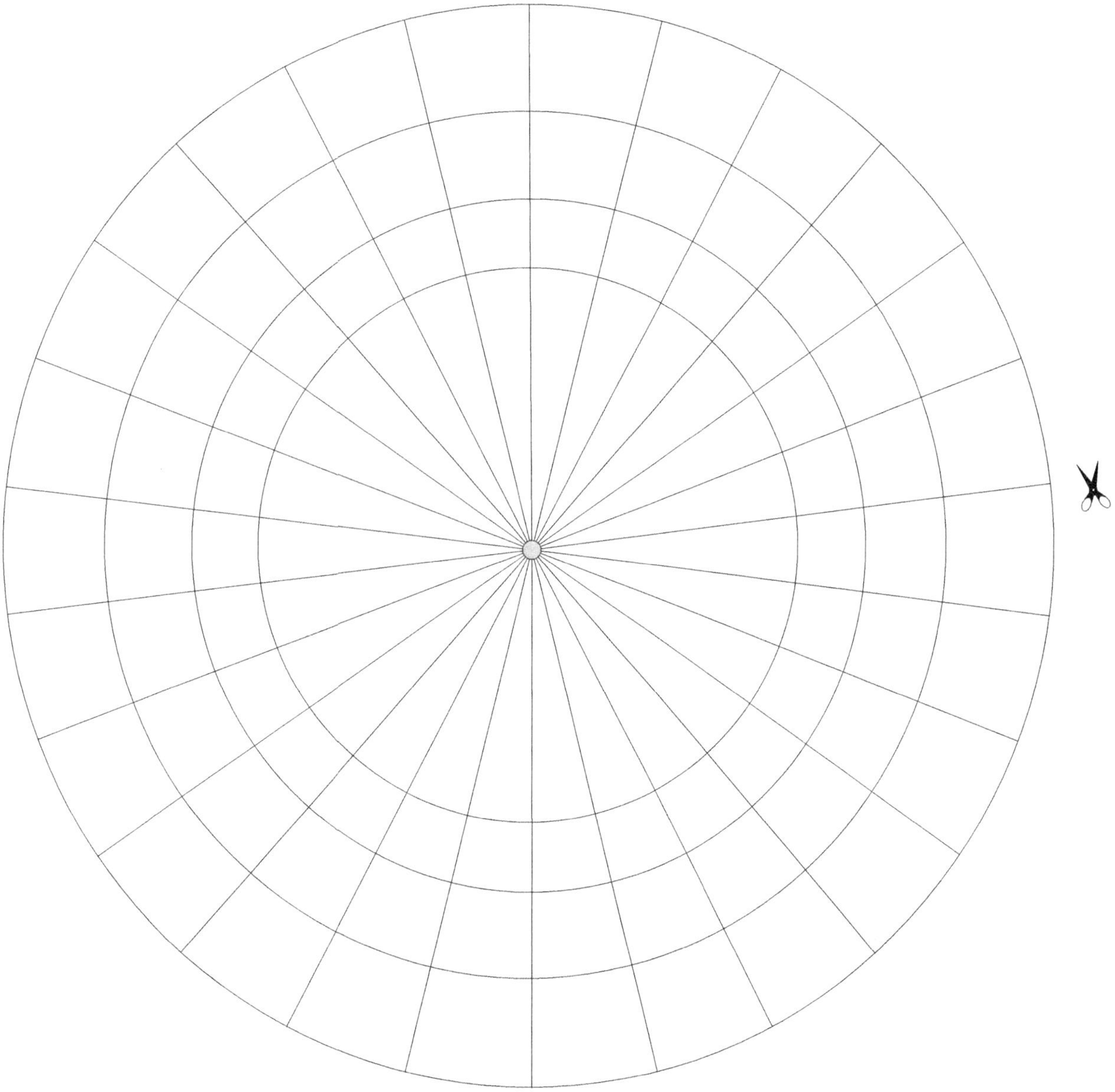

Template.1 (Large circle)
Make your own secret wheel

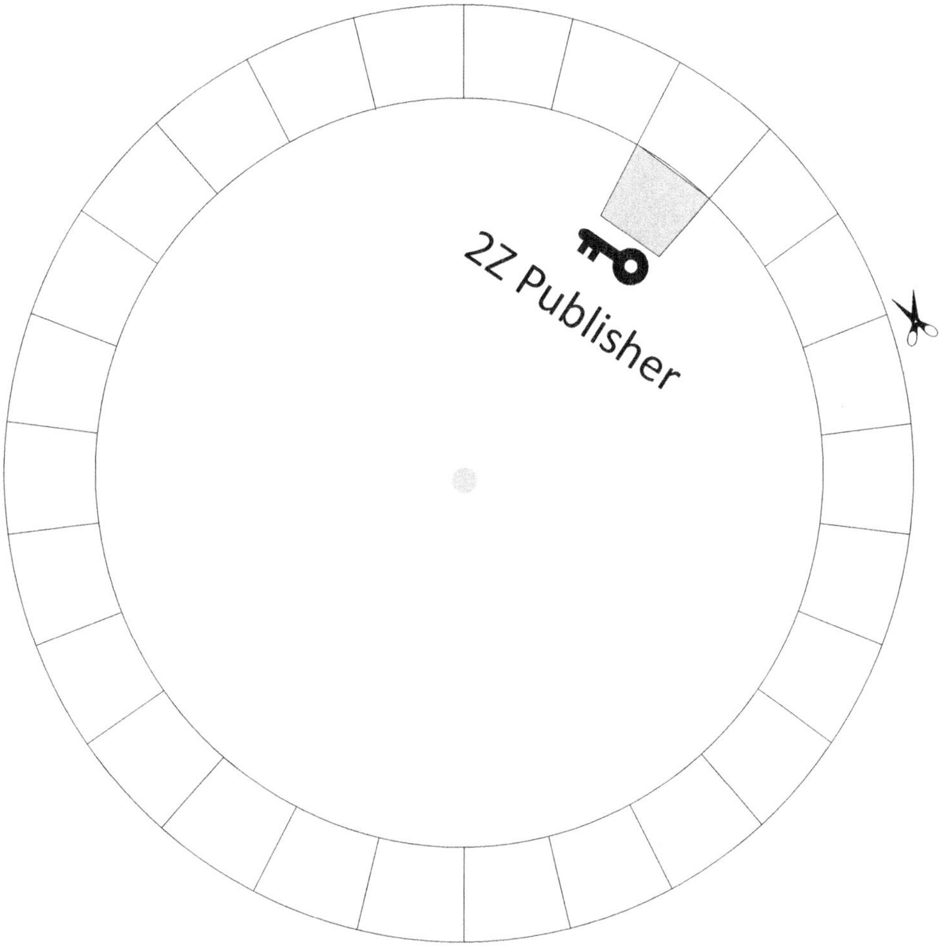

Template.2 (Small circle)
Make your own secret wheel

The **2Z Publisher** team Hopes

that you enjoyed this book.

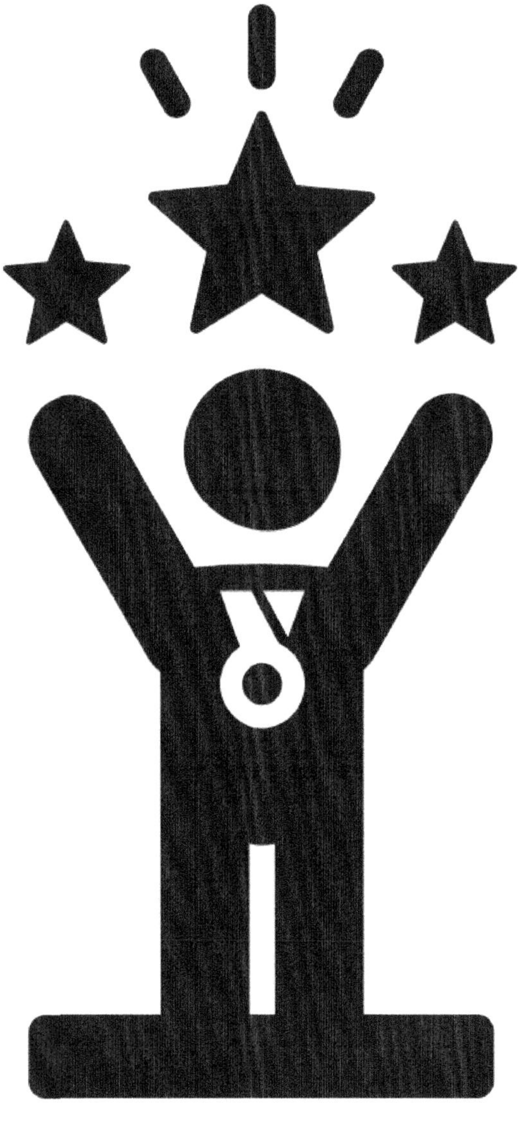

We would really love to get your **review** and positive feedback on Amazon.

2Z Publisher

..--- --..   .--. ..- -... .-.. .. ..-.

Write your memoirs in a secret way using one of our products as (Notebook: Morse Code Secret Notebook) form 2Z Publisher.

Practice Morse Code using one of our practice sheets as (Morse Code Practice Notebook).

2Z Publisher has many books about Morse code and other coding methods.

Visit our Page on AMAZON by scanning the QR code, using the next URL, or searching with "2Z Publisher" in the Amazon search engine for more info.

amazon.com/author/2zpublisher

What's Your Story?

Tell us your story about learning Morse code as you can inspire others to learn.
We would really love to get your **review** and feedback on Amazon.

Thanks for your trust in our products.

2Z Publisher
..--- --..

Printed in Great Britain
by Amazon

54748168R00084